Aging in the Lord

by

MARY HESTER VALENTINE, SSND

PAULIST PRESS
New York / Mahwah, N.J.

ACKNOWLEDGMENTS

The Publisher gratefully acknowledges use of the following materials: excerpts from "One Jesuit's Spiritual Journey," by Pedro Arrupe, S.J., and "Of Many Things," by George W. Hunt, both published in *America,* February 16, 1991; reprinted with permission of America Press, Inc. 106 West 56th Street, New York, NY 10019; copyright © 1991. All Rights Reserved. The photograph on the cover is courtesy of Giraudon/Art Resource, NY; "Two Female Heads," by Albrecht Dürer, Musée Condé, Chantilly, France.

Library of Congress Cataloging-in-Publication Data

Valentine, Mary Hester.
    Aging in the Lord/by Mary Hester Valentine.
      p. cm.
    ISBN 0-8091-3486-1 (paper)
    1. Aged—Religious life. 2. Aging—Religious aspects—Christianity.
    I. Title.
BV4580. V35 1994
248.8′5—dc20   94-16327
                                         CIP

Published by Paulist Press
997 Macarthur Blvd.
Mahwah, N.J. 07430

Printed and bound in the United States of America

Contents

No one lives for oneself,
and no one dies for oneself.
For if we live, we live for the Lord,
and if we die, we die for the Lord;
whether we live or whether we die,
we are the Lord's
Romans 14; 7–8

To Doctors
Gregory J. Topetzes,
Gerald J. Dorff,
Kesavan Kutty,
David J. Mathias,
and the many nurses who keep me vertical.

Why This Book Was Written

Aging is inevitable if one lives long enough. Like the poor, the old are always with us, as is the specter of our own age always in the wings waiting for its turn on stage. What is interesting is that younger children accept the old with little difficulty; they relate to them easily, and the differences between them produce no problems. Those who see their own age on the horizon have greater difficulty dealing with its evidence.

Our age, however, can be ignored and protected against for only so long; sooner or later we are caught in the web of years, and are forced to allow ourselves to be as old as we are. Our society is basically anti-old, although with the graying of America that may change. Now, negative phrases describing the elderly are an indication of a lack of esteem. We are old codgers, old fogeys, old bags, old nags, or the reverse images which are equally patronizing: little old lady, or dear old man. To the federal government we are senior citizens, a title which accompanies retirement and Medicare benefits.

The question, of course, is: How old is old? The chronological boundaries are as fluid as the individual moving within the time span. An accumulation of years is a weak indicator of change. Age norms and expectations depend upon individual physical and mental abilities, as well as the cultural and, unfortunately for many, the economic and social context. Since most of us resist being stereotyped, at the same time that we recognize how common

1

such overall categorizations are, we tend to view advancing years with mixed feelings.

The double entry nature of aging is obvious in much of current literature, reflecting as it does the contemporary attitude. Some geriatric research confirms the emphasis on the negative aspects, focusing on sickness, limited resources, whether financial or social, isolation, diminishment and subsequent shattering of the sense of personal integrity. Other studies emphasize the positive in equally unrealistic fashion. The happy, white-haired golfer, the eighty-year old mountain climber, the grinning shuffleboard players in the senior day-care center give as one-sided a picture as does media emphasis on older residents burned out of their homes, the frightful conditions in some nursing homes, or an ambulance loading the elderly mugging victim.

Commercials present a similarly mixed picture of aging. Age is most visible in ads for health and food, less so for style, appliances, cars or household products, unless these are designed for the handicapped. One positive image of age in commercials is that it is frequently a symbol of quality and wisdom. Travel agencies are realizing a potential market in the elderly, and have begun to advertise group tours with less strenuous schedules, a shorter travel day, and more comfortable accommodations.

There is no question that various social patterns exist at the end of the twentieth century that make growing old more difficult than in earlier times, or in some other cultures even today. Our forebears, if the records are valid, apparently knew how to revere, care for, and honor the elderly in ways that seem to be substantially forgotten today. Previous generations accepted their old; grandparents frequently lived with younger members of the family. But we must be wary of imputing blame on contemporary young people. Circumstances of living are not always subject to control. One of the contributing facts which makes inter-generational living more difficult today, it seems to me, is the size of our homes. Larger houses gave breathing space; when proximity rubbed human relationships there were escape areas. Today's smaller houses crowd family members into constant, and sometimes abrasive, relationships.

I remember my own grandfather, usually a mild-mannered man, for whom a build-up of pressure occasionally reached explosion point. He would race up the stairs to his room, slam the door so vehemently that it seemed to shake the house, only to emerge a respectable time later, his customary, pleasant, controlled self. These episodes never frightened anyone, for we knew from experience that everything would be all right. Grandpa's house had space; I do not know where tensions today find release in the small modern apartment. All this is simply to underscore the fact that we ought not to blame today's young for conditions over which they have no control.

It is true that some cultures still demonstrate unusual respect for their aged. When I taught in Korea I learned that in that country only two birthdays are celebrated: the first, to rejoice that the baby has survived the dangerous first year, and the sixtieth, at which time one becomes a living ancestor, to be given the respect due to experience and the wisdom it is presumed the years have produced.

Men who have achieved this august state wear a special white suit and a black high hat, while women have colors reserved for them. Universal respect is assured, even from strangers. While I have admiration for this custom and similar recognition in other cultures, I am an American, and I relate most comfortably to my own tradition. I refuse to be lured into rejection of the here and now, even though it may produce problems that another time or country does not face. Those of us for whom more of life is in the past than can be realistically projected to the future need to be constantly aware that facts do not automatically add up to truth. Our human existence is richer than can be captured by any number of news stories, statistics or research projects. From the moment of our conception life is graced by God, and he does not limit his gifts to our active years. Looking back we can see how times of difficulty were actually the rich garnering periods. The years of diminishment can also bring moments in which God is closer than he ever was in our busy, time-clock pressured years. The realization is that most of us are uncomfortable about physical aging because it must ultimately lead to death. And because much of physical aging is decremental, we may fear that death will be preceded by a lengthy period of physical and mental misery.

The problem for most of us is that although we know that the only way to avoid old age is to die young, we do not consciously advert to our own advancing years until a sudden illness or a retirement notice forces us to face the reality of our personal vulnerability. Someone has compared our life span to two trains: one the moment of our birth, the other the moment of death. From the time we first draw breath these trains are rushing toward each other, but it is not until they are very near the collision point that most of us face this, our human condition and its time boundaries.

This book has grown out of my own experience of aging, an experience which has been both incremental and sudden. I knew the adage, "After seventy-five it is downhill all the way." But for me it wasn't. It took a critical illness and what a doctor euphemistically called "a fragile clinical picture" to force me to face the reality, not that there was no going back, but that it would be impossible for me to maintain the measured life I had been living so actively and happily. I am fortunate. I had time to plan my retirement, to finish some writing to which I was committed, to dispose of the academic shards of forty years of teaching, to set a date for leaving the old familiar places and for entering a whole new life with my peers. There were particular psychological needs and stresses that are normal to this special stage of development, but the affection of the friends I was leaving, and the warm welcome of those I was joining, helped to make the pain of loss less raw than it might have been, and that it is for so many who do not have my supports.

During the months of preparation for my transfer to this, the last stage of my earthly journey, I read as much as I could find about the problems of retirement: what I might expect to find in myself and in my companions, and how to deal with difficulties which would inevitably crop up. Much was interesting and informative, but with few exceptions, notably Karl Rahner, Teilhard de Chardin, May Sarton, Czeslaw Milosz, all of whom wrote from the high mountain of their years, the authors were young professional gerontologists. They wrote with knowledge, and frequently with sympathy, but always from the viewpoint of the observer. It became more and more obvious to me as I lived the separation from the past, and moved into my precarious now-time, that there are some things that cannot be taught; they can only be bitterly experienced. That is an awesome truth for which there is no sedative, but for which honesty carries some balm. Answers are inadequate when the questions have not even been asked. I have learned that there is a beautiful, blessed side to aging, but there is also a terrible side, when the body announces with finality, "I can no more." It is then that platitudinous, easy phrases fall with a sickening drop. They carry no comfort. Part of the pain lies in the fact that it is so personal; there is no way by which the emotional crisis can be communicated. And most of us have no desire to share this most personal, intimate kind of suffering. We shut the door firmly against proffered sympathy, and close well-wishers out. Silence can sometimes mean rejection as well as resignation. It may also be the manifestation of a reluctance or perhaps the inability to deal with the unknown and untraveled.

It is the life-altering dimension of this life crisis which demands so many decisions and changes that I found unsatisfactory in much of what I read. I did not react as strongly as Betty Friedan, who notes wryly that the gerontologists talk about "them, the aging, the feeble objects of care," saying, "We should give them every possible say so, but we do ultimately have to decide." I share with Miss Friedan the uncomfortable thought that I have become one of "them," for whom decisions are about to be made.

While it is painful to move beyond denial and to accept aging in oneself as an affirmative development, it is necessary, for it is only acceptance that frees us of our terror of the fact. But no amount of encouragement from the young can touch the inner core of the pain. That was my problem as I read voraciously.

People have been writing about old age for as long as there have been writers. But Cicero, who wrote *De Senectute* in pre-Christian Rome, would not have been old enough to collect Social Security had there been any. Robert Browning, who glorified old age with the familiar, "Grow old along with me/the best is yet to be/the last of life for which the first was made," may have had some doubts about that youthful encomium at the end of his life, and Shakespeare, whose descriptions of the physical aspects of age in *Henry IV*, "a moist eye, a dry hand, a yellow cheek, a white beard ... voice broken, wind short," is accurate enough, but it does not touch the inner man. The terrible play, *King Lear* in which the suffering of the mad old king is a universal picture, is a marvelous rendition of the stereotype of powerlessness, lack of control, senility. But then, Shakespeare died before he reached sixty. How could he know the reality?

The personal meaning of aging is most profoundly shaped by our direct experience of it, in contrast to what it means in our culture, to the professionals in the field, or to people in general. It was this realization that impelled me to write this book. It may say nothing that has not been noted by gerontologists. The difference, if there be any, will lie in the fact that what I say will be from the vantage point of experience, other than the chapter on death and dying, which I obviously have not experienced, although I have observed it all too often.

I am an old woman. I retired first from full-time to part-time teaching, and writing, several years ago, and moved into this full-time health-care center this year. But each older person is an individual, as are people in any other age group. I respect this uniqueness, and I do not expect to cover the multiple facets of that stage of life when we are face to face with our mortality. I do, however, hope to touch the more common changes associated with aging: the adjustment to diminishing strength and health, to reduced finances, to retirement, to coming to terms with limitations, to the increasing loss of those we love in death. I will touch on how aging affects our use of time, our leisure, our friendship, our faith. I remember with a smile the advice given me by my grandmother when my life was without limit, and mortality but a word. She recommended me to always have some younger friends and older friends in order that I might avoid loneliness and be challenged by the different perspectives on life. It was a sound rule, but if one lives long enough there comes a time when one is the last leaf on the tree. And will loneliness set in then?

Not necessarily. Thank God, not necessarily, for as St. Paul said, "Nothing can come between us and the love of

God." This friend, who never grows old, can become closer at the end of our lives than he has ever been before. We
have time to communicate with him, and we also have
time to listen to him speak in the small and larger issues of
our life. He can fill our days so that there is no emptiness,
and we sometimes wonder that it took us so long to experience him like this, realizing that soon we shall know him
as he is. Teilhard pointed out that God must in some way
or other make room for himself, hollowing us out and
emptying us if he is finally to penetrate into us. If we per-
severe courageously we will meet God across evil, deeper
down than evil, and draw close to him. God ordains the
cross and death, and all those things that "ought not to
be."

In this book I hope to face frankly the physical aspects
of age, the diminishment which results, the quite real
problems the elderly must confront, sometimes with the
help of relatives and friends, but even then, and perhaps
especially then, alone, since sharing pain can put a burden
on others the elderly do not want to impose. I will try to
suggest ways by which we can deal with our frailty, some of
which I have personally found useful, some of which others have found valuable. These are our final years, and as
Dear Abby advised a correspondent, they are supposed to
be the golden years. We ought to keep them shining.

Retirement years can be the richest of our lives. Studies
have shown not only that we live longer than our predeces-
sors, but that we enjoy considerably better health, and certainly easier living conditions. The capacity for enjoyment
of each day increases as we recognize it for the gift that it
is. The freedom to pursue activities which a crowded work
schedule had not permitted can be its own delight. Some
take up hobbies long neglected, some who live close to colleges and universities attend classes and forge new friendships with new interests. My own college recently graduat-

ed a seventy-six year old woman at whose commencement her classmates rose in spontaneous tribute to her enthusiasm and example. Some develop long neglected talents, even begin small businesses, join volunteer groups in hospitals, nursing homes, rescue centers or teach in language schools for immigrants.

Not everyone, obviously, has the physical capacity for strenuous activities, but there are quieter and equally pleasant alternatives—reading, visiting, listening to music or producing one's own. I recently attended a concert given by an orchestra made up entirely of senior citizens. The possibilities are limited only by one's desire and circumstances, and I will make suggestions about possible things to do and places to go in subsequent chapters.

But I am no Pollyanna. All is not sweetness and light, and it would be dishonest to pretend it is. No one is served by a refusal to accept the fact that, as Hopkins said, "Hold them cheap may, who ne'er hung there." What I hope to share, however, is the increasing certitude that I am experiencing that pain can heal as well as hurt. That prayer in pain reaches God, and as Teilhard de Chardin insisted, "suffering becomes a visit and caress of God." We come to experience what we have always known—that God who holds our future and our past never asks of us more than we can bear. As someone has said, "He may be slow in answering our prayer, but he always does. He is never too late."

We learn how effective prayer is because it is not we who pray, but the Holy Spirit who speaks "with unspeakable groaning." If we are willing to believe we recognize that these groanings are joined to ours; rather, our groanings become one in the Spirit. Our lives are safe in God. With Chardin we can learn to assimilate, to utilize the shadows of later life: "Enfeeblement, loneliness, the sense that no further horizons lie ahead. Discover in Christ."

I do not know all the answers to the questions that the aged face, but I am learning the only way, through experience. Jung has pointed out that in the later half of life we tend to turn inward. It is an examination of life, and an acceptance of it. Our disengagement is necessary for a successful adaptation, and as we are stripped, one by one, not only of things we held dear, but of the very physical and psychic qualities on which we have depended, ours becomes Socrates' examined life and well worth living. We discover that our hierarchy of values slips from the seen to the unseen.

It is out of the growing awareness of these beliefs that this book has been conceived. It will deal with the negatives, surely, for they are all too real, but it will also deal with ways many have developed to handle the problems that face the aging in our society, and the special awareness of the timeless when time is rationed, the increasing relationship with God whose name is Love.

This book, then, is written for all those who share with me the excitement and challenge of growing old with all its insights and blindness. It is also addressed to anyone who expects to grow old.

When We Face the Inevitable

There comes a time for everyone when the inevitable must be faced. We awaken one day to the realization that we have gradually been adjusting our lives to the physical shifts occurring in our bodies. Most of us cannot identify when we first experienced functional changes; we made subtle compensation unconsciously. We use the elevator oftener, think twice about running out to the drug store, and prefer daytime driving to facing the oncoming headlights at night.

My first realization that the years were limiting my freedom of movement came to me when I was teaching in Seoul, Korea. The university at which I taught was at the top of a small mountain, and the volunteer house where I lived was at the bottom. The twice-a-day trek up the mountain was a wonderful stimulus to memory, for before I went up in the morning I deliberated seriously about what I would need for the day. I realized I was not a light-hearted or light-footed mountain goat. Forgetting a book or set of papers could precipitate a small crisis.

A group of senior citizens were comparing when they became aware that they had slipped into the ranks of the elderly. One remembered as small boy telling his mother, "Let the old ladies go first, mama," as she and two friends queued at the theater box office. Another recalled a clerk at McDonald's sliding change across the counter, assessing accurately that she was eligible for a senior citizen discount. A third told of a waitress bringing a senior citizen menu, and a fourth told of a knowledge conveyed by the first social security check. A teacher added, "I used to say, 'A hundred years ago when I was young,' until I saw that the students weren't laughing anymore." The youngest, a mere fifty-nine year old, added quietly, "I was jolted last Sunday when the Lenten regulations were announced. I realized that I no longer have to fast."

Chronological age and its effect on health are not uniform. All of us know people younger than we who are much frailer, and an equal number of older people who seem endowed with limitless energy that we no longer have. Social security classifies us all as senior citizens with eligibility for Medicare and full retirement benefits. While few people enjoy the prospect, most recognize that the increasing difficulty they feel in responding to the pressure of work indicates that slowing down is no longer an option but a necessity. Physical indications are obvious: climbing a flight of stairs brings on shortness of breath, voices are not so clear as they once were, and we have difficulty recalling names. We make little lists of important deadlines lest we forget.

Each of our body's systems and organs is on a slightly different schedule for maturation, duration of maturity, and the onset and rate of aging, and each person's own timetable is individualized. Studies have shown that although muscle strength remains relatively constant through age seventy, the volume of oxygen that can be gotten into the bloodstream is only about half as much as at age forty. As a result, the amount of work most of us can comfortably perform declines, although the ability to practice existing skills may remain stable. Recovery from exertion takes longer; chronic illness becomes more prevalent, and vision and hearing begin to decline. Although a continuity of lifestyle and habits ensures the ability to cope, there comes a point for everyone at which a reassessment of what we are doing and why is urgent. The functioning of our minds and bodies is affected by aging in many ways. It alters the amount of energy we can mobilize, affects our stature (we shrink), alters our physical appearance, and increases our susceptibility to "the ills that flesh is heir to."

Fries and Grapo of the Stanford School of Medicine, who have done in-depth studies of vitality and aging, stress that no diet, vitamins, drugs or tonics extend the human lifespan, although a sensible regimen can help maintain normal health for the individual for many years. Their studies emphasize that "there's nothing that keeps its youth but a tree and truth." So, for all of us there comes that moment of truth: I am moving into old age; what will I do with my remaining years? Disability is not automatically a part of the aging process, but its possibility must be faced.

It is not an easy confrontation, for the irreversible physiological and sometimes psychological deterioration that accompanies age is difficult to contemplate. The high point of our lives is still to come, the mystery of God into which we are falling. We are no longer in control. We never were, actually, but a busy, active life may have hidden this reality. The knowledge of our powerlessness can come suddenly, and for serenity to triumph the realization must be linked with the firm conviction that now as in the past, underneath are the everlasting arms. What makes this time especially difficult is the fact that there is no rite of passage from the active, productive life to the period of lessening involvement, and there are few role models. The unanswerable questions loom large, and for some these are faced for the first time, leading to depression and a depletion of emotional resources. Suddenly they are faced with a disillusionment with life, an experience perhaps of not having accomplished much, in spite of years.

Job, so far as we know, was not an old man, but his cry

to God "Why? Why?" has run down through the ages. A comic strip is not usually the jump-off spot to contemplation, but recently Hagar the Horrible carried a strong message. Hagar is at the foot of a mountain crying out, "Why me?" a lightning bolt carries the thunderous response, "Why not?"

John Donne affirmed that no man is an island, and while in the context of his poem he is right, there are other barren areas of life when each one is truly an island. Facing our own aging self is one of these times, and we face it alone always. Family and friends may want to rally around, to give us encouragement and support, but the stripping of the occupation, surroundings, companions who have made life a pleasant journey, and eventually the elements of our very personhood are too individual a deprivation to be shared. The Irish have a saying, "To each man his own sorrow," and this is particularly true at the end of life.

How then do people manage. How is it that we do see so many obviously happy, well-adjusted elderly men and women, if aging is such an emotionally draining experience? How do they make life an adventure as long as it lasts?

Without denying the painful diminishments that occur at this time, it is also true that, like riding a bicycle downhill, the descending years of our lives can be exhilarating and challenging. Aging is a natural human process like any other, and if understood and reinforced emotionally and spiritually, it can be a positive period of growth. Adjusting our lifestyle to the limitations imposed by age does not mean we must become hermits. The new freedom from a time-controlled day can actually release our creativity for new, purposeful activities. Karl Rahner, who defines happiness in terms of satisfying human relationships and mental activities which transcend physical discomfort, added that he did not consider this to be an old man's euphoria or serene retrospection.

Matilda Riley, a gerontologist, who at eighty-one still puts in a full day in the National Institute on Aging, sees more and more choices and varied roles for older people in our society where lifelong learning replaces the lockstep of traditional development. Milton Berle advises seniors to achieve renewed interest in life. Betty Friedan urges the elderly: "Get on with it; getting older is an adventure, not a problem."

Seeing the ridiculous in unexpected happenings helps. Mary Bender of Winona, Minnesota, was amused recently when she received an invitation to attend kindergarten along with others who were born in '88. She isn't going, though. She entered the world in 1888. "Boy, wouldn't those kids be surprised if they saw me coming to school," said Bender, now 105 years old.

Clinical psychologist Thomas Cottle points out that what we do defines our identity, but that does not necessarily require us to be gainfully employed. There comes a time when our gifts are no longer marketable, but that does not mean we cannot enrich our surroundings. In a later chapter I will make some suggestions of ways by which the elderly can keep their own lives green while benefiting others. But for now I would like to continue to dwell on the means by which we deal with the realization that our life must change direction, that while today is the sum of all our yesterdays, our tomorrow must be lived today.

It is Rahner, again, who points the way. In his own old age he asked, "Why should I ever doubt that a boundless, incomprehensible, eternal mystery, which carried all reality in its origin, still surrounds me?" We exist in transcendence beyond every imaginable circumstance, and are moving toward reality. It is the realization that this is so, even when we experience no evidence, that enables us to accept the passivities, the things we undergo in contrast to the days when we made the decisions for our lives. The entire life cycle is the revelation of God. A friend who recently underwent serious surgery corrected a visitor's wry "feeling your mortality?" with "No, our immortality."

Carrotti tells us that God touches us in our flesh because the tears issuing from that flesh teach us how to mature in the things of God. His love is terrible when he has a mind to save us. God truly waits for us on the way. In fact, he actually advances to meet us. I recently saw a picture of a young woman in a path running toward the shadow of her lover cast forward. The girl is a symbol of each of us, and as we move forward to the end-time, God is also moving toward us with deliberate speed. What a wonderful meeting that will be. Seen from our point of view the active occupies first place because we prefer it, and because it is the more easily perceived. But in reality, the passive is immeasurably the wider and deeper part.

In our quiet time, then, in our prayer time, there is the power to charge the world with the divine influence. It is what happens within a person during these less physically demanding times that changes everything. It is when we rest in God that we receive unmeasured resources of dignity and courage to face the unknown. It is in understanding that God works in our lives, so that it is not only to him, but with him that we say our inmost yes. In all the galling diminishment that being human involves, in all the doubt as to what lies ahead, there is still the strong recognition that while we do not know what the future holds, we do know who holds the future. If he has watched over our past he will not desert us when we are most vulnerable. In him we live and move and have our being, and that is comfort enough—most of the time!

I do not want to fall into the trap of offering too easy a

comfort. Someone has noted that the wintry climate cannot be overcome by simply proclaiming high ideals and acting as if they could be realized with a little good will. There is no way to make aging simple, nor is there any one pattern by which it can be recognized. It is probably the most complex period of life, and between the young-old, those in their sixties and early seventies, and the old-old, those eighty and older, there are vast differences. Many newly retired find beginning a new life to be challenging, and they anticipate a number of productive years. For other elderly, there is no denying the fact that the final decades of life are a long history of suffering on many levels. We ought not to mouth lofty principles while people are in pain. As a friend noted, "Until now, no matter how bad things got, I had my health. Now that has gone, and I need health insurance."

Illness strikes the aging when they are most vulnerable and when inner resources to endure seem in short supply. Their financial situation is suddenly threateningly precarious; loneliness sets in as friends and relatives die or move away, or they themselves become incapacitated. As a result they feel that their world is falling apart. When haunted by these ultimates many answers to life's ambiguity are frightfully inadequate. I believe it is Rilke who tells us not to seek the answers now, but to live the questions.

Not long ago I was brought up sharply to a recognition of the danger inherent in a too-smooth assumption. I had been impressed with a fantasy exercise in Fr. De Mello's *Sadhana*, and was explaining it to a physician friend. De Mello suggests that we are to imagine ourselves paralyzed from the neck down, and he recommends that we think not of what we could not do in those circumstances, but what we could, in order to thank God for the gifts of sight, hearing, taste, thought, love.

My physician friend listened, and then said, "Don't try

telling that to a paraplegic." It brought my own fantasizing up short, for I knew what he meant. It is easy, all too easy, to ignore the reality of suffering when it is the other person. I believe it was Yogi Berra who said, "You don't feel my pain." Fortunately for us, Jesus, who holds every moment of our lives, does feel our pain, and helps us to bear it.

While it is true that for many the later years are lived under shadows, this is not a universal experience. Studies have shown that the majority of the older population are able to adjust lifestyles to the conditions of life. By accommodating to the limitations the years have imposed, they find pleasure in doing the possible rather than regretting the impossible. With a relaxed attitude they approach each day as a special gift. The expression "on borrowed time" for them has a positive rather than a negative meaning, and they treasure the sacrament of the moment, happy to be able to function within the parameters they themselves have set. To recognize that satisfaction in activity is not measured by an external standard, but by positive personal autonomy, is energizing in itself. There are many opportunities for stretching horizons, both physical and material, and the next chapter will touch on some of them.

Golda Meir summarized one approach when she quipped that old age is like a plane flying through a storm. Once you are aboard there is nothing you can do. I think Rabbi Heschel's wisdom would be a good addition: "These are formative years, rich in possibilities to unlearn the follies of a lifetime, to see through the in-bred self-deception, to deepen understanding and compassion." Faith, then, is the foundation on which the graced years rest, faith that God who gave us life still sustains us. We are old because he wills us to be, and although we cannot see the reason, there is one. His is the plan, and as Cardinal Newman said, "He knows what he is about."

When We Retire

The number of old-old Americans is on the increase, according to the Metropolitan Life Insurance Company. By their definition, the old-old are individuals over the age of eighty-five. In 1990 there were 858,000 men, and 2.22 million women, age eighty-five or over. There were also 21.2 million people age sixty-five or over. These numbers are expected to increase dramatically, so that by the middle of the next generation it is projected that America will boast 78.9 million people over age sixty-five, and 17.7 million over eighty-five.

Millions of Americans are obviously in the retirement age bracket. Like age itself it is an eventuality everyone faces. For most of our lives we think of it as something in the far future. Young adults perceive it in a vaguely favorable way as a time when work will not be expected of them, but they also prefer to think about it as not pertaining to themselves. The older worker, however, views it as a distinct possibility. The way he deals with the prospect has a significant bearing on what life will be like when that day finally arrives.

People of all occupations and professions retire. It is interesting to note that while Supreme Court judges are appointed for life, some opt for retirement—in the recent past Thurgood Marshall and Byron White, for example. Priests are ordained to be priests "forever according to the order of Melchisidech," but they are expected to retire, nevertheless, and for bishops it is mandatory. Only one pope has ever retired: Clement, and Dante placed him in hell, probably for cowardice in leaving the scene of political conflict. Amusingly enough, we know him as Pope Saint Clement, canonized for not presuming to do the impossible.

Retirement for those who plan for the change appears to be smoother than for those whose jobs are terminated suddenly, or for whom declining health makes work difficult if not impossible. Defined officially as the institutionalized separation of an individual from his occupational position, like all jargon it does not take into consideration all the human issues involved. While retirement does demand a withdrawal from some social and communal activities, and from active responsibility for many productive work-based roles, it can also be an enriching period of life.

Some leave the work world voluntarily, and take early retirement in order to experience some years of leisure while they are still young enough to enjoy it. The high degree of self-determination that characterizes retirement can exert a substantial pull, even for people who feel effective in their work. Studies show that by the end of six months most people who freely plan their retirement have settled into a routine of activities that is satisfying and long-lasting. But planned retirement involves practical preparation, and for many this is a difficult decision to make, and even more difficult to implement.

When the moment of actual decision comes it is natural to have sudden reservations. One wonders whether, in a time of economic upheaval, it is prudent to sell the business or the house, whether financial resources are adequate for the unforeseeable future, or whether one is carrying sufficient insurance to cover catastrophic illness. At this stage of life such considerations are not only usual but practical. A recent study of the American Medical

Association concluded that the majority of American citizens have at least one chronic disease by the age of forty, two by the age of fifty, three at sixty, four at seventy, and at least five after that scriptural end-point. These are even spelled out so that we can check our own health by that gauge: heart and lung disease, hypertension, arthritis, and diabetes are the more usual.

It is to be expected, then, that a plan to retire is fraught with questions, even when there is the nagging conviction that it is the thing to be done. The problem is that we have no experience of this kind of definitive detachment from the physical and relational ties that have made up our lives. For no other of life's passages is finality so built in. Our decision in late adolescence to continue our education or to join the work force was made with our entire future as the objective. Our choice of profession rested on the twin props of given talent and future prospects. Our vocational choice carried the same forward-looking vision. Retirement lacks the long vista; even for those who choose it there is less of beginning and more of ending. For this reason many gerontologists feel that this may be the most crucial life change to which individuals ever have to adjust.

I have often wondered why spiritual retreats are not scheduled for those planning to retire. St. Ignatius considers his Spiritual Exercises important for those making a choice at a decisive point in one's life, and certainly the grace and logic of existential knowledge gained in prayer at this serious decision point of life would be advantageous. But even without the structure of a retreat, prayer at this time would be valid.

At some point the actual decision to retire has to be made, a decision which is always accompanied by a certain uncertainty and darkness, and a vague doubt as to the wisdom of our choice. For most of us it also involves many other people: spouse, children, employer, fellow workers, friends and relatives. On a practical scale, preparation ought to begin long before the actual severance process. In today's world all who can do so take out retirement insurance, join pension plans, put aside part of their earnings in the form of savings. Some sell their large family-oriented homes and rent smaller utility apartments close to shopping and recreational facilities; some move in with siblings, children or other retirees to help incomes stretch to cover the future.

Decisions both small and large must be made: what to keep, to give away, to sort, to pack. The disposal of a lifetime of memory-laden objects can be painful. The uninvolved observer may wonder at final choices. I remember overhearing a young woman question her widowed mother, "Why do you want to keep all this old stuff?" The mother's answer struck me as a summation of the unspoken needs of all the elderly, "My dear, what I have is valuable because it is all I have."

For some, the disposal of carefully gathered possessions carries a special hurt. Garage sales and auctions mean that treasures will belong to people for whom they carry no wealth of memories. I was witness some months ago to the quickly covered pain in the eyes of a man whose daughter did not want her parents' lovely early American furniture because, as she said with finality, "But Dad, our home is contemporary Danish." She was sensible, of course; the tables, desk and chairs would not have fit into her decor. But what her rejection said to her father was that these tangible evidences of his past no longer had meaning.

I suggest that in these dark days of divestment we might turn to our Lady for strength not to succumb to destructive self-pity. She understands what we cannot express, for she experienced similar renunciations. After the death of Jesus she lived with St. John, leaving the little home in Nazareth where every stone spoke of busy, happy days with her husband and Son. And if tradition be true, she traveled far away from the warm, familiar hills of Galilee to distant Ephesus. Oh yes, she understands retirement well.

Since people are living longer than they used to, and one-third of the average American's adult life will be spent in retirement, this anticipating and planning for the change is crucial. For many, family help is available. There are also agencies that provide services, and social agencies usually have lists available. The American Association for Retired Persons provides regional lists to its members. Helpers usually function on two assumptions: assist the capable or help the helpless. In most situations either assumption is valid, but when neither applies, additional guidelines may be needed.

It would be unrealistic not to admit that economic security is a cushion for the retired: it enables one to make choice of a lifestyle, environment, travel possibilities, entertainment, all of which provide a sense of well-being. An elderly wag on a radio talk show commented recently that how the retired fare individually depends upon luck, money, and genetic inheritance.

There are senior adult communities in all price ranges in Florida, Arizona, and California. The best provide the advantages of a private club, and at about the same price. We have all seen ads with the healthy wealthy riding their golf carts from their nearby luxury apartments, conveniently situated near their banks and boutiques. But there are also more reasonably priced facilities which provide meal preparation, light housekeeping, and transportation to medical appointments, beauty and barber shops, and religious services. Some have medical supervision, rehabilitation and supportive therapy when these are needed.

In planning retirement a survey of potential living arrangements should have top priority, unless one does not expect to change residence, the most satisfactory arrangement if it is possible to maintain. So long as people are in familiar environments, skills and knowledge developed from long acquaintance with the immediate surroundings can be used to compensate for lessening functioning. Our past does blend with and become a part of our present, and there is a consistency in maintaining a known situation. Only when confronted with new people or significant environmental change do most of us become aware that age may have reduced the capacity to cope quickly with new situations.

One of the reasons retirement communities in Sunland have had such a phenomenal success is that they play upon another of our human needs, related to the familiar: groups from a single geographic area are urged to come together. Friends are major factors in selecting a new environment for many. Immigrants know this; it accounts for the national clusters in our cities as well as concentration of national groups in some states: Scandinavians in Minnesota and the Dakotas, Germans in Wisconsin and Pennsylvania, Mexicans in the southwest.

Some retirees plan vacations for years before they stop working. While travel may place financial limitations on extensive use, for those who can afford the expense, travel is no longer considered a problem for the elderly, if it ever was. It is an enriching way to make the break from a work program to leisure. Dr. Daniel Warren believes there are very few reasons why the elderly or those with chronic conditions cannot travel. With an adequate supply of prescription medication, a current list signed by a physician to prevent questions about carrying illegal substances, and medical emergency insurance, which most tour operators offer, older citizens can plan to travel almost anywhere.

There is a caution, however. A ship's doctor commented that while older Americans may be admired for their spunk, these tourists can be just as easily criticized for their folly in traveling the world over with often very significant and sometimes uncontrolled illness and severe disability. In any case, it is wise to check a guided tour program before signing up, for while tours eliminate the problem of hotel reservations, transportation, and tickets for events, they also sometimes tend to crowd too much into a day or night. While senior citizens are not children, and can indicate they do not intend to participate in all scheduled events, most are happier with built-in rest periods. There are tours on the market planned for and limited to the older generation, some even under the Elderhostel aegis.

Personally planned travel can be exciting in both preparation and achievement. By dividing a trip into small components with rest and recuperation at a base, fatigue can be kept at a minimum. Having a focus can be fun, too. Greyhound has discovered this, as has Amtrak; both sponsor historical tours, visits to literary spots, and theater weekends. A personally planned vacation provides for individualized interests and needs. I recall a retired relative who, with his wife, did a "dinner tour," from the midwest to the east coast and back, enjoying all the area delicacies from northern Michigan pastries to southern Maryland crabcakes. They acquired a lot of practical geography and history on the trip, too. The holiday was successful because they had planned carefully to minimize the physically taxing aspects; all reservations had been made and confirmed, distances for each day spaced to allow for plenty of rest, visits with friends and relatives along the trail, and any exploring that might beckon. Although their energy, strength and endurance were limited, they returned from the holiday rejuvenated and not exhausted.

Such personally planned trips provide flexibility, and adapt to personal preference and physical capability. One pattern some have worked out to their own satisfaction is to decide on a central place to use as a base, usually a small town or suburb within commuting distance to the area they plan to explore. From this focal point they take short trips to nearby spots of interest. The advantage is that they unpack only once, settle in, and return to a familiar spot.

House exchange can be a satisfying experience, but is best arranged between close friends or through an agency that specializes in such swaps of residence. Some senior citizens join with a number of others traveling together in a kind of modern-day caravan for a sense of security, moving together to previously agreed-upon spots.

All of these are the happy scenarios, and are not available to everyone, since financial restraints and physical disability limit the majority of senior citizens. Senator Tom Harkin of Iowa spoke to this problem, saying, "Some would have you believe that most Americans nearing retirement are getting ready to head to Palm Beach for evening cocktails at the club. But studies show how vulnerable millions of elder Americans are to declining health and income. For them the peace of mind we all want is replaced with insecurity and worry." The Department of Health and Human Services in 1990 published some sobering statistics. Of one hundred Americans who have careers, by age sixty-five, more than half—fifty-five—have incomes between $4,400 and $29,000, the median income being $6,9800. Thirteen have incomes under $4,400, that is, below the poverty level; only three have annual incomes over $29,000, considered as the level for financial success, and twenty-nine are dead.

For the greater number of us, then, retirement means adapting to reduced financial resources, learning to make do with less. Aging affects income in ways that were not even considered in an earlier era. While the amount of money needed for transportation to work, special clothing for business, or meals away from home may be reduced, increased physical frailty increases the need to buy services that formerly could have been done by oneself. Expenses mount up. Household maintenance, food, clothing, medical and dental care, pharmaceuticals, laundry, cleaning, grooming, insurance, taxes—all produce an alarming pile of bills at a time when income is fixed. A not yet retired relative of mine recently sold his home and moved into a smaller house, because, he said, he and his wife concluded that maintenance, taxes, heat, electricity, and insurance for the house cost them more per month than they were spending upon themselves. They were restricting their own activities, entertainment, recreation, sometimes even debating about special food, all to take care of the house.

His divestment was a free choice. But often senior citizens have constraints that force them to move. As long as they can, they try to maintain themselves in familiar surroundings to support a sense of identity. Independence and personal effectiveness support self-esteem at any age, but this capacity to influence the conditions of life is especially valuable when the parameters of living are narrowed.

There are senior adult communities with one or two bedrooms with on-site dining, bank, convenience stores, indoor parking and supportive services and companionship. Such arrangements are likely to have ramps, widened doorways to accommodate wheelchairs, or sturdy hand support fixtures in the bath. This, obviously, provides an active retirement with comfort, self-respect, freedom and peace of mind.

A balance between independence and the assistance becomes crucial as the years wear away strength and mobility. The share-a-home concept has offered a viable alternative for those who need semi-independent housing.

Each family hires a cook and a housekeeper, thus avoiding problems of having to divide housekeeping among people of varying physical capacity. Companionship encourages a healthy lifestyle.

Retirement communities also foster social interaction, but the majority of these draw their residents from the more affluent social classes. Mobile home parks abound, but are a mixed blessing. Natural disasters such as Hurricane Andrew and the Mississippi floods of 1993 have demonstrated the unreliability of trailer homes to withstand the elements and the difficulty that senior citizens may have in leaving threatened areas in an emergency.

There are reliable resources available for information, although too often those who need assistance most are unaware of these. The Older Americans Comprehensive Service Amendment of 1973 created a community organization, the Area Agency on Aging, AAA, which brought new priorities on coordination of services and on planning. Social service agencies have lists of groups serving specific needs, and usually one's doctor can make relevant recommendations. The telephone directory groups available resources under special categories. A five-minute check in my own local telephone directory was revealing. Under Government Offices, I found Departments on Aging, Senior Citizens, Human Services, Senior Centers, Blood Pressure Programs, Medical Benefits, Health Centers, Nursing, and Public Health, gratifying in their implications, sometimes amusing. There was a number for assistance when there is a lack of heat or electricity, another for holes in the streets, another for defective sidewalks. Numbers for nuisances included noisy neighbors and barking dogs. There are, admittedly, huge gaps in concern for the aged, but it is clear that more effort is being made by government to bridge the gaps than is usually realized.

Social services for the retired consist of a broad range of often unrelated programs that revolve around the general goal of helping people get the things they want. These may include family services, the foster grandparent program, talking books, meals-on-wheels, and employment and protective services. I recently saw an ad in our local paper for a Smart Shoppers service. It shops on order, and delivers medicine, household items, and clothing, all for a flat fee per trip plus ten percent of the purchase.

Another business provides personal care including sewing and mending. There are attorneys who specialize in the legal needs of the elderly with wills and other legal papers prepared in the home. Neighborhood restaurants will sometimes agree to deliver meals on a monthly basis. I know two older women who have made use of this service, ordering from the restaurant's regular menu, and paying by check at the end of the month.

Many communities have senior centers which take the form of private non-profit corporations, often underwritten with United Way money. The average multi-purpose senior center adopts a flexible program, one that involves informal companionship, crafts, hobbies, artistic activities and music. Enjoyment of leisure is the focus for many such programs.

The more creative have a variety of offerings. One church day-care center has a news group whose participants have visual impairments that make reading difficult. One of the assistants at the center reads the paper to these at a regular hour each day. Coffee and cards afterward provide opportunity for discussion in a casual non-confrontational setting.

Performing arts centers frequently make a block of tickets available to senior citizen groups, so concerts, ballet, and theater are potential sources of entertainment. However, lack of transportation can limit participation in such outreach programs. I recall a retired engineer remarking with matter-of-fact realism, "They tell me to get out more. I don't drive now; I can't handle the steps on a bus and can't afford a taxi. My children have their own families, and in any case are working when the programs at the center are offered." This man is representative of a large number of retired, whose independence is similarly limited. Statistics have shown that less than half the older population owns an automobile. The same study showed that while most were still able to get to the doctor, dentist, grocery and drug stores, they do not to go see friends and relatives or to church. When they do, it is usually at someone's expense. Pride and a sense of dignity often prevents them from asking relatives or friends on any but rare occasions. As a result, while their basic needs are being met, the larger human inter-relationships which give meaning and value to life are severely restricted. "I'm starting to feel a little irrelevant and a little obsolete," remarked one house-bound friend.

Recently I had occasion to visit a retired professor, a former colleague, whose sight and hearing are severely impaired. She is fairly independent, lives alone by choice, and several times a week a visiting nurse checks on her condition. She can no longer read, and neither TV nor radio gets through the physical barriers of encroaching blindness and deafness. So, with the exception of an occasional visitor, she is very much alone. A salty, independent character, she is coping reasonably well. But after I left her I reflected on the fact that the penal system and prisoners themselves consider "solitary," one of the most severe disciplinary actions, one reserved for incorrigible and unusually dangerous criminals. Even these fear the "hole," with the strain it places on the frail thread of sanity. My friend lives in almost complete solitude, a prisoner of her own years.

But there is no disintegration of personality; her own comment on the situation revealed why she is so serene, so completely in control. She said to me before I left, "Now I know what St. Paul meant when he said that we make up in our bodies what is lacking in the sufferings of Christ. Did it ever strike you that Jesus was a young man when he was crucified, and that horrible though that death was, he never experienced the gradual depletion of old age." She added quietly, "He lets me make up that deficiency in the redemptive plan. That's rather awesome, you know." I found her awesome.

One of the restrictions that many elderly find especially trying is that which limits their attendance at church services. For years communal worship was an important part of their lives. Now distance, difficulty in transportation, and, for some, the architectural problems presented by steep stairs make even Sunday services difficult, and, in inclement weather, impossible. Someone has pointed out that many churches that emphasize programs for adolescents and young families lack similar programs for older people. While most churches are quite willing passively to accept the participation of older people in church affairs, there is little effort actively to solicit their participation. There are exceptions, of course. I know of one parish in which younger members are paired with older parishioners, and the relationships, which have grown into friendships, mean that older partners are picked up for Mass, and are taken to meetings in which they become active contributors. The church lobby has a bulletin listing the parish sick, hospitalized or housebound, and next to each name is a space for a parishioner to sign, assuring that during that week someone will visit. Usually, of course, the visitor will be a friend, but the important thing is that individuals are not allowed to drop from living memory in that parish. In this time of acute priest shortage such responsibility of the people of God for each other reflects the communities of the early church described in Acts. This interdependence is an expression and affirmation of the Christian bond of love about which we talk so often. For the young, responsibility becomes an enriching experience; for the elderly, dependence becomes a grace, binding belief and life.

There is much more that could be said about retirement. Like all of life, it eludes categorizing. The problem is that at every stage of life the experience of the individual differs. Many older adults have found the quality of their lives improving in many ways. About twenty percent of those who retire experience an overall decrease in activity, but this decrease is sometimes welcome. It may be a real relief not to have to keep up the pace of the work-oriented world; this is especially true if one retires for health reasons. While some psychiatric studies of the elderly are fairly negative it is good to remember that rarely do psychiatrists deal with people who are not having adjustment problems. A goodly number of the retired are doing nicely, thank you, and are committed to an active lifestyle, some even from wheelchairs.

In the next chapter I will talk about the possible avenues for growth at the end of life, and some of the services even the handicapped can render. I remember a story told of Cary Grant who was filming in Great Britain. A writer for a popular magazine, doing a feature on Grant, wanted to know the actor's age. To save money he scrimped on words in the cable which read, "How old Cary Grant?" The actor cabled back, "Old Cary Grant fine, how you?"

It is with some of the senior citizens, who, like Grant, are just "fine," that the next chapter will deal.

When We Contribute to Society

Once the initial excitement of retirement has worn off, and the realization that every day is as free as a holiday begins to slip into monotony, many elderly, especially those in reasonably good health, look around for something challenging with which to fill the days. Most of us are not hedonists, and unlimited leisure soon palls.

This chapter will describe a number of older people who have refused to let the years rob them of their productivity; most of them are Americans, most of them are still active.

I have had some hesitation about writing this, for I have personally experienced the frustration of an uncooperative body, and the subconscious sense of guilt when reading about others similarly handicapped, or even more seriously disadvantaged, who somehow continue to function as contributing members of society. It is important at any age, and particularly in the final decades of life, to admire others, but to live easily with oneself and one's limitations. I believe it was Francis de Sales who noted that some saints are to be admired, others imitated.

Some of the people I shall write about, then, deserve our respect, but to be depressed because we cannot emulate them is as foolish as to resent Annie Scott, Scotland's oldest citizen, who turned 110 on March 16, 1993, or Jeannie Calment of Arles, France, who, if *U.S. News and World Report* is to be believed, turned 118 in February 1993.

Adult identity in the United States is very strongly tied to the capacity to be independent and personally effective. While there is no norm by which it can be measured, I wonder what there is in the artistic temperament which enables these gifted persons to continue creating well past the time when most of us have eased off into a more passive lifestyle. There is the Spanish artist, Esteban Vicente, for instance, who arrived on his ninetieth birthday for the show at the Berry-Hill Galleries in New York, entitled "Esteban Vicente: Five Decades of Work," in March 1993. For more than two hours he stood in the crush of the opening reception crowd, greeting people, making jokes and answering questions. Several days later, interviewed in his studio on West 42nd Street, to which he commutes, he said, "I paint every day; there is no way to avoid it. If you don't paint, you do nothing." The interviewer noted that Vicente conveys a sense of mystery possessed by individuals who reach a great age and yet continue to pursue their vocations with vigor, perhaps even increased vigor. In fact, critics believe he may be doing the strongest work of his career now.

Then there is George Pollard, official portrait artist for the Milwaukee Brewers and Milwaukee Bucks, who, at seventy-three, was commissioned to paint Pope John Paul for a World Youth poster, and Dorothy Stratton, eighty-four, who recently arranged her show at the Wesley Palms gallery in San Diego, saying, "I would like to reach out to stir an interest in the visual arts." Asked if artists ever retire, she answered, "Never! Never!"

Winston Churchill, an amateur artist as well as a statesman, told a friend as he carefully painted a landscape, "Life begins at eighty. The only thing I fear is dying of boredom."

In my retirement home there are several sisters whose paintings are of professional quality, although until they came here they had done nothing like it. "I was always too busy," remarked one, a former teacher and elementary school principal. "I started to paint when I was eighty-five; you can say I changed my profession then," she adds with a smile.

Musicians usually peak early, but the best of them continue to give delight long after their late recordings do not compare with their earlier magic. One thinks of Pablo Casals, of Vladimir Horowitz, of Yehudi Menuhin, all of whom felt they had been given a gift for which they were responsible, and for whom giving joy was finding joy.

Even amateurs seem to possess and spread this pleasure. John Goulet, an eighty year old resident of Milwaukee Catholic Home, is an accomplished pianist and published composer who made his living in advertising. At one time he played with the Prince Ballet Orchestra in New Mexico, and with the Starlighters Orchestra in Colorado. Now his enjoyment is to share his "not so nimble fingers" with fellow residents.

And then there is Bob Hope whose ninetieth birthday gala on May 29, 1993 brought near centenarian George Burns to the party to salute him. Hildegarde still sings, as does Johnny Cash.

The growing number of retired have shown considerable political power, and the so-called Gray Lobby is a measure of their success. Part of the ability to resist age discrimination results from the existence of large national organizations of older people. The National Retired Teachers Association and the American Association of Retired Persons have memberships of over six million age sixty-five or over. The Gerontological Society of America represents about five thousand professionals whose research, teaching and practice involves aging or the aged. The National Council on the Aging represents over one thousand agencies that serve the aged, and all of these organizations have banded together to form a leadership coalition of organizations.

One reason why older members of political parties and those in government are influential is the weight that tenure carries in politics compared to other types of groups. In government the older person often plays the role of sage. The retirement of Supreme Court Justice Byron White in the summer of 1993 drew attention to other active members of that body who have exceeded the scriptural threescore years and ten: Harry Blackmun, eighty-four, and John Paul Stevens, seventy-two. Judge Elbert P. Tuttle of Atlanta, Georgia, is now ninety-five. He is still senior judge for the 11th Circuit Court of Appeals in Atlanta, and he continues to work daily at the court-house named after him on Forsyth Street. "I plan to be there until I breathe my last breath," the judge said. He and two other judges screen cases each day to determine whether they should be considered for review.

There is a group of lawyers in Los Angeles who give advice in legal matters to other elderly, and a retired banker assists with the muddle of Medicare forms.

While doctors seem to have a more limited time span of professional life, a local hospital recently honored an eighty year old obstetrician who has delivered thousands of babies. Dr. Benjamin Spock recently celebrated his ninetieth birthday in an appropriate setting, "Boston's Biggest Baby Fair." Leland C. Clark, Jr., seventy-four, believes he is on the verge of a breakthrough that could have far-reaching medical implications: synthetic blood. It would give patients access to inexpensive, easy-to-store, universally compatible blood. His laboratory is at Antioch College in southwestern Ohio. Dr. Clark is no dreamer; more than 75,000 open-heart surgeons every year use Clark's principles for oxygenating blood; his was the first heart-lung machine used in open-heart surgery.

Veterinarians long have respected ninety-five year old Dr. Elmer A. Woelffer who admits he has cut down, but still has about a dozen farms in as many states, where he serves as a consultant. He has won enough awards, citations and trophies to cover the side of a barn, and hopes to raise the number of four million cattle examined to five million, "If I keep going."

It isn't only men who continue performing efficiently into old age. Rear Admiral Grace Hopper stayed on active duty until she was seventy-nine years old. I have a ninety-two year old friend, a former bank official, who after retirement was invited to join a travel agency where she was a hot commodity because of her travel experiences. Confined to her home now because of bone problems, her spirit and enthusiasm for life remain undiminished.

Authors continue to write even into old age. James Michener is currently doing research in Russia, I understand, for a book on the recently publicized American POW's there; Eudora Welty and May Sarton, both octogenarians, continue to write, almost as if racing some invisible time clock, and Muriel Spark has just published her autobiography because she was disturbed by the errors in current biographies. Nobel prize-winning poet, Czeslaw Milosz, eighty-two, has a poem every other month or so in the *New Yorker*. In fact, you frequently see the names but do not know the age, and it doesn't matter. Their writings stand on their own merit, but for us whose age parallels theirs it is encouragement of a sort. My own feeling is probably a reflection of this: "If God gives me strength to write in old age I can accept it as a gift, not as a reason for self-congratulations." Many authors say that it is an opportunity to sum up one's entire life before the final mystery.

Innumerable older people participate in a variety of types of volunteer work in almost every community. The Retired Senior Volunteer Program (RSVP) helps by providing transportation to and from the place of service. The program is active in schools, hospitals, courts, day-care centers, nursing homes and a host of other organizations.

Marcie Koenigs began her career as an election inspector twenty years before Bill Clinton was born, in 1928. This year's presidential election was her last, after sixty-five years of manning the ballot box. "After all, when you get to be eighty-five years old, you've put in your service," she said.

Marian Remberget, eighty, who works in an outpatient program for addicts and alcoholics, recently cut back to a six day week. "Now I take Sunday's off," she said. "I work other days until I am not needed."

Colette Oberembt, seventy-one, a retired social worker, is on the board of directors of Transitional Living Services, which serves people who have been discharged from mental hospitals, and of the Planning Council for Health and Human Services in Milwaukee, which evaluates social service programs. She recently completed a three-year term as a committee member for the Campaign for Human Development which required her to read and listen to presentations of groups seeking funding, but also to travel to see in action the work for which funds were being sought. "There are exciting and hopeful things going on," she said, and she is part of them.

Many senior citizens serve independently or in a group with friends. In California several seniors gather produce from farms which, because it does not conform to regulations for size, cannot be sold; they distribute it to the sick, the elderly and the needy. Another group runs a food pantry stocked with donations, a typical work that is repeated in many cities. Retired men and women bag groceries, check the expiration dates of products, and make decisions about where the food goes. Elizabeth Bany, seventy-eight, one of these dedicated volunteers, says, "One of the things I've learned is not to judge anybody. If people ask for food, we can't ask all kinds of questions."

A retired friend learned that neither a law nor a medical degree was needed to be a legal guardian for those not competent to make financial and medical decisions for themselves. Compassion and a sense of commitment are the prime attributes that the Legal Aid Society seeks in volunteers for its Guardian Advocacy Instruction project. The staff provides guardianship training, supervision, and support for volunteers. Once enrolled and trained, volunteers provide friendship and assistance, not financial support or daily care, to those who need help. A serious commitment is involved, and that the retired can give.

Public TV recently did a documentary on a group of retired men in Massachusetts who recondition furniture and toys, do woodwork, and repair electrical equipment and household articles which have been thrown out or are left over after garage sales. The finished products are given to Goodwill, St. Vincent de Paul and other service organizations, including the parish churches of the group. What began as a hobby in one of the men's basement has so expanded in both gifted members of the group, and in work to be done, that they now rent space in the inner city, where they deal directly with their "customers." They were obviously having such fun that their envious wives set up their own resource center, where they teach sewing, cooking, home nursing, and English in an adjoining storefront. They have added a gimmick to their husbands' "We serve" philosophy; they invite the women who live in the neighborhood to help. Many of these older women have untapped skills, creating beautiful clothing for children and babies, and when word got around of the exquisite workmanship the place was crowded with would-be buyers. It was amusing to see the chagrin when it was explained that nothing was for sale; everything was destined for distribution at local centers.

An expansion of the dual Mr.-Mrs. project is the center for adults with special needs: the handicapped and disabled. With contributed service from the Visiting Nurses Association and local hospitals, an adjoining empty building is used as a day-care center for the otherwise housebound. Older people in the neighborhood have been taught special skills. Through the enterprising efforts of one of the women the Senior Companion Program was invited to visit, and now offers a small, welcome stipend to the helpers.

One of the original retirees when interviewed remarked, "Well, we never thought it would grow this big. We were bored doing nothing, and it seemed like a good thing to do. Good for everybody." He added reflectively, "Good for us especially."

A more formal organization using similar capabilities is the Service Corps of Retired Executives, which offers retired businessmen and women an opportunity to help owners of small business and managers of community organizations who are having management problems. I knew the manager of a paper mill in Upper Michigan who, on retirement, went with his wife to spend six months helping a fledgling paper mill in South Korea use modern equipment. He called it his Peace Corps stint.

The Foster Grandparent program employs low income older persons to help provide personal, individual care to children who live in institutions. It is of benefit both to the older people involved and to the children they care for. Many older people in the program report feelings of increased vigor and youthfulness, of a sense of personal worth, of a renewed sense of purpose and direction in life.

Volunteers have a high degree of life satisfaction that does seem to make a difference in maintaining continued vital interest in living. Those involved in community service practice an unself-conscious altruism in which they see their own needs in a context that includes the needs of others. A friend, who as a successful business woman traveled all over the world, is now engaged in so many volunteer situations that she is busier than ever. She is a part-time librarian in a hospital, a relief switchboard operator in a retirement home, on the governing board of her condominium, a member of her parish council, and an advisor to a young divorced woman.

Some retired businessmen and women have found satisfaction in teaching, some as guest lecturers in colleges and universities, some in vocational and high schools as a kind of contributed brain trust. Former teachers tutor in learning centers, and the increased number of non-English-speaking immigrants makes experienced teachers very welcome. Wisdom gives these volunteers perspectives that are invaluable.

Many senior citizens take advantage of the reduced tuition or free auditing privileges to attend interesting courses in colleges and universities. Today the older student is a familiar part of any class. I have a friend, an internationally known toxicologist, who, as a hobby, is finishing work for a Ph.D. in English literature. He has persuaded the department in the state university to allow him to satisfy the dissertation requirement with a medical study of the famous missionary to the lepers, Fr. Damien. One of the professors told me that classes in which the doctor was registered are always at a high level, since he set a standard of excellence other students aspired to.

Some schools, like my own college, have established a special department designed to meet the needs and interests of the older students as they explore, change and grow. There are programs for personal effectiveness in developing a home-based business, the use of computers, and creating publications with graphics. Some are geared for spiritual growth, some for physical wellness. Cultural enrichment includes foreign languages, history, contemporary problems, book reviews, art and writing courses. It is a rich offering and one available almost anywhere there is a technical or liberal arts college or university.

Federally sponsored Elderhostels offer an interesting variety of programs on selected campuses with distinguished professors opening doors to continued learning.

Going to school is obviously not exclusively for the young anymore.

While the example of these energetic people can be an inspiration, it would be wrong for us who cannot presume to such high levels of activity to conclude that we have nothing to contribute. Aside from the fact that our worth as human beings does not depend upon our achievements, there are many ways by which our horizons can be broadened. Crisis prevention institutes can always use qualified individuals who do telephone counseling and assist with a helpline. Samaritan Service has evidence that a listening ear can, on occasion, be the difference, literally, between life and death. Potential suicides have been averted and the despondent directed to support groups by individuals manning phones from their own home.

Letter writing is a real apostolate, an activity that can be pursued in the privacy of one's own home and at one's own pace. Prisons can supply lists of inmates who would benefit from correspondence, as will juvenile and nursing homes where a personal letter is an event. Amnesty International, which has a remarkable record of achievement in mitigating the cruelty, torture and injustice in the world, depends to a large degree upon the millions of letters of protest of its members. Membership is not expensive, and bulletins keep one aware of the places where intervention may have a positive impact.

There are smaller opportunities closer to home which are often neglected. A word of praise for a taxi driver who successfully maneuvers a difficult intersection, the organist who plays a favorite hymn on a Sunday morning, the child who sets a table with care—all respond with surprised pleasure to a word of commendation.

A warm word of thanks can bring a smile from a harassed clerk or a delivery boy. One tends to think that gratitude is an automatic response among civilized human beings, but such is not always the case. I recall my shock when the distinguished orthopedic surgeon who had performed a delicate operation successfully answered my thanks with the smiling comment that he appreciated my appreciation because "People so seldom express thanks. I suppose they figure they pay my bill and that is enough." It is sobering to remember that most of us receive more personal care than we actually pay for; gratitude to the person providing it is in order. This, of course, does not mean an effusive, fulsome approach to the ordinary aspects of life, but an awareness of the graciousness which not only makes daily living easier, but is an expression of Christian inter-relationship.

Jonathan Swift said long ago that every man desires to live long, but no man would be old. We can take a different view, for these later years are the fullness and deepening of earlier stages of growth, a time of ever new discoveries of God's world and the kindness with which he has surrounded us. If we do not build a wall around ourselves, the world still spreads out before us, even if the parameters are narrow.

Each of us has a mission to accomplish in the name of Christ. We have no way of knowing when the important moment may arrive. Perhaps it will come in these twilight years. Responsible initiative allows us to weave the texture of our days. Life does not need to become less precious as one grows older; it just becomes less cluttered. May Sarton made an important observation when she said, "I tend to forget how important the empty days are," but I would like to add, "only if the emptiness is not of our own devising."

This chapter, I hope, has suggested some ways by which the days may be filled and the deadly apathy engendered by the sense of defeat at the end of life avoided. One last hint: a rereading of Matthew 25:35-40 will be a reminder of how many things we can still do, even in old age, that will give evidence that we are friends of Christ.

When Emotions Surface

When I told an eighty year old friend I was including a chapter on the emotional life of the elderly in this book, she looked at me quizzically, and made the amused comment: "The emotional life of *this* elderly is the same it has always been, only more so." She was saying in effect what psychologists have long known: the pattern of aging is essentially the same as that followed throughout life.

Emotions have always been tricky areas to handle, because they are powerful psychic movements. It is even difficult to discuss them unemotionally, rationally. Two major attitudes creep into any such discussion, one that sees them all as intense and violent in the areas of sexuality and anger, and one which sees them as the basis of all value and productive action: love, joy, courage. But our emotions in the golden years, as certainly as in any others, are essentially neutral. No moral judgments can be made about our feelings, only on our reactions to them.

Immanuel Kant considered all human emotion as pathological (an attitude I find pathological!), but Thomas Aquinas insists that emotions, which spring from our yearning for happiness, are simply not a matter of free choice; we crave happiness by our very nature. And that is good news for us emotional older citizens.

Love as a word today is pompous. We have over-used it on banners, bumper stickers, T-shirts, to the degree that it actually means little. When we love smoked salmon, warm weather, Beethoven's Ninth Symphony, our family, friends, and God, the word if not the relationship fades into no meaning.

In this final decade of the century it is impossible to speak of love without reference to its sexual components, since our news, our entertainment, our social emphasis is on that area. I am hesitant to discuss this aspect, since marriage, with its joys, crises, sorrows, its agony and ecstasy, has not been a part of my life. I do have married friends my own age, and while we feel free to run the gamut of our interests in conversation, their sexual life has never entered into our sharing.

Dr. David Barash, of the University of Washington, holds that old age brings changes in sex life just as it does in other respects, but he stresses that these changes are not dramatic and certainly not catastrophic. Older people cement bonds of love and affection at the same time that they forge new ones. They find warmth in mutual appreciation. All our lives, even into old age, we need others, and need to know that others need us.

Donald Goergen reminds us that gentleness and tenderness are rooted in human sexuality, and that compassion is a supreme sign of a well-integrated life, sexual or otherwise. Ensley, discussing prayer that heals our emotions, points out that sexuality involves much more than intercourse. Every time we experience the warmth of affection toward God, toward family, toward creation, we experience our sexuality.

How do the elderly measure up to these standards? The evidence says, "Very well."

Chief Justice Holmes' classical remark on seeing a pretty girl, "Oh, to be eighty again," underscores the fact that emotions do not become less with the years. Scott Maxwell's, "My eighties are passionate; I grow more intense with age," could be repeated by hundreds of octogenarians. But this is not a contemporary phenomenon.

St. John Climacus wrote, "A certain man, seeing a woman of unusual beauty, glorified the creator for her; the mere sight of her moved him to love God." An older nun, a contemporary of mine, said recently with a twinkle, "When I was young I 'guarded my eyes'; now I admire the beauty of the young fire-fighter who gave the lecture." A man celebrating sixty years of marriage told a young reporter, "Hers is the face I'll be happy to look at for the rest of my life. I'm grateful to have found her."

In a recent issue of *Time* (September 27, 1993) two marriages were noted: that of Amy Carter, twenty-five, daughter of former president Jimmy Carter, and Loretta Young, eighty, movie and TV star, to Jean Louis, eighty-four, Oscar-winning costume designer. That ought to say something about the agelessness of love.

Today when the divorce rate is rising steadily, it is good to be reminded of love that withstands the wearing of the years, of married couples for whom the wedding promise, "for richer for poorer, in sickness and in health," has meaning a half-century later. Harold Barkowitz of North Miami Beach, Florida, a seventy-two year old retired orthopedic shoe repairman, made the news recently. For the past six years he has given his wife, Rosalyn, sixty-seven, who has advanced multiple sclerosis, an extraordinary amount of TLC. He has cooked for her, dressed her, mended her clothes, bathed her and carried her from room to room. His story is just one of many the Clinton health care program has brought to public notice. Stories of caring love which have surfaced, like that of Barkowitz, indicate that devotion and compassion are still motivating factors in family life. A young student of mine said, "I don't remember my parents ever using the word 'love' in relation to themselves or to us children, but they lived it."

I heard last month of an older man whose wife died in an accident in which both had been involved. He insisted on attending her funeral, even though it meant his hospitalization might be extended because of the physical strain. His grief needed to be shared so that it could be borne. Fortunately the doctors and hospital staff were open to his emotional need. He had lost so much he had to be allowed to be in control of this small decision.

I have a friend whose husband, suffering from Alzheimers, still warns with concern, "Take care driving home," when she leaves him after each hospital visit. We have all heard of love so strong that it communicates across the miles. My own family has a treasured memory of such a distance-spanning love. My grandmother, attending her youngest daughter's concert several miles from her home, a performance grandpa was unable to attend because of an important business conference, suddenly rose. She left her seat in the middle of a brilliant piano concerto, pushing her way to get to a phone. "Something is wrong with Will," she whispered to her puzzled sister, who was sitting on the aisle. She was right. Something was terribly wrong. Her husband of forty years had died suddenly of a heart attack. There had been no warning, no banshee wail, but grandma knew. You may call it ESP, mental telepathy, or simply a love that reached past the miles to say farewell.

Without human affection we deteriorate. One hears occasionally of health care personnel who do not understand this basic truth when it applies to the elderly. Only comparatively recently have nursing homes provided accommodations for the married couple. I remember years ago visiting "an old folks' home" with a student choir, and the appalled reaction of the young visitors when they learned that they were to entertain the men and women in separate rooms. Only last month I heard of a caretaker in a nursing home who made the devastating comment that wheelchair patients were the least troublesome at a party. "The others sometimes get carried away and can present problems." Her problem was with couples sharing a paper, watching TV together, talking, or perhaps slowly and warmly falling in love—a totally unacceptable situation.

This is not a universal reaction, of course, for most nursing homes accept reality. The frequent announcement of late marriages in local newspapers is evidence that loving relationships are not always discouraged. Some elderly couples are closer in their declining years than they have ever been, communicating on many levels and continually finding new things to share. The unusual and dramatic are publicized, but there are countless other marriages whose apparently ordinary, humdrum life is suffused with a courageous love. Their pleasure is simply in being together.

The heart, as someone has said, is not sexual, and there is the love of friendship, too. I remember Dan Herr in a lecture insisting that since we are gendered individuals every relationship is in some way sexual, but not necessarily genital. Erik Erikson's famous life-span theory changed when he himself reached eighty. At that point in his life he stressed the fact that in old age, identity is defined by feeling, intuitions, intimacy, tenderness, and coming to terms with love. Commitment, dedication, and a shared experience are part of the precious gift of friendship.

Psychologists point out that those who love are more likely to be loved in return, and evidence bears this out. This past year I lived with two elderly nuns who had worked together for over thirty years, and their friendship was a joy to witness. When one died rather unexpectedly, her friend was understandably numb with grief and loss. One day I met her on a path outside the house; she had just been to the cemetery to visit her friend's grave. "I tripped," she said, smiling, "but Sophie steadied me before I fell." Who is to say her dear dead friend did not?

Protecting and preventing injury are attributes of a love-relationship that may well bridge time and eternity.

Courage, enthusiasm and self-confidence appear to be significant emotional facts in any adjustment in critical life stages, not the least of which are one's final decades. This week I visited a remarkable ninety-five year old nun who told me that this year she is not making so many fruit cakes for Christmas, "only a couple of hundred for the development office and the faculty." She added quickly, "Do you want one?" Hers has been a lifetime rich in adventurous giving, and the end is no different. I found her some weeks ago preparing the college president's dining room for a board of directors' dinner. My spontaneous thought was, "She's wonderful." But she would reject that label; it only underscores the stereotype that make competence and caring in the old unusual. She does not categorize others in that fashion, and would not appreciate my doing so to her.

As we age we establish new intimacies to replace those time has stripped from us. Grandchildren are among the solid pleasures. Reeve Lindbergh believes that "the relationship between grandparents and grandchildren may be so wonderful because little children have just come from the infinite, and we who are old are approaching it, and somehow there is a kind of recognition." Fantasy? Perhaps, but there is no arguing away the relationship.

The quick bonding between the young and old goes beyond the ties of blood. Watch an older person hold a baby and the relaxed pleasure of both. Smitten with each other, there is eye-to-eye contact in love. This past year a primary teacher in a neighborhood school asked the sisters in our retirement home if we would be interested in becoming "pen pals" with her first graders who were learning to write. I accepted the invitation and was linked up with a charming little boy whose letters always ended with, "I love you, I love you, I love you," surrounded by hearts. At a bingo party scheduled for the end of the school year I watched another small boy and his white-haired partner play two cards. Whoever filled his first slid the card across, and the "winner" smiled in delighted conspiracy and raised a hand. At the same party I overheard a six year old ask her wheelchair partner "Have you ever been old before?" to which my peer answered, "No, have you ever been little before?" and they both grinned acknowledgement of the absurdity.

Our capacity for emotion grows with advancing years. How much does a child really love in spite of carefully lettered protestations? Love is not an easy virtue; loving the poor, the lonely, the hurting of the world takes courage. It is considerably more than feeling; it demands involvement. Mother Teresa of Calcutta has long been an example. In the fall of 1993, leaving the hospital after angioplasty she expressed gratitude to God, to the doctors, and to the hospital because now, at eighty-three, she could go to China to open a house for the sick poor.

The essential self is ageless. André Gide wrote, "My heart has remained so young that I have a continual feeling of playing a part." Being old does not necessarily mean being bored. There are public events to celebrate, the unique gift of each day to enjoy, the beauty of the changing seasons to admire. The old, being human, grieve over accidents, not only those of family or fiends, but the ones which fill the news: plane crashes, train wrecks, earthquakes, floods, fires, terrorist strikes, the incredible multiplication of homicides in cities. And they love baptisms and weddings.

Days take on emotional overtones they never had before: Christmas, when the infinite became finite; Easter, the special feast day of hope for the old. A ten year old recently asked why his religious education teacher had told them that Easter was a bigger feast than Christmas. Of course he cannot grasp its wonder; given time he will, he will.

There can be an emotional downside to holidays, too, because they are family days. I was struck a few years ago when I caught an elderly friend perusing his address book on Christmas. "I always ask myself on days like this who is the lonesomest person I know, and then I call him." He himself lived alone after the death of his wife, but apparently had maintained warm inter-personal relationships with lives that touched his, so that he himself was not lonely.

Not everyone is so self-reliant. Recently I heard an old man tell a visitor "There isn't a living soul who knows me as I am. The children call me Grandpa, my son calls me Dad, my landlord calls me Mr. Elkin, but no one calls me Dick."

For some there is the tension between the desire to share in-depth conversation with a close friend, and the physical exhaustion that just being with people brings. The consuming loss of a spouse is not always through death. A woman grieves for a husband whose physical disability has cut off communication that sustained them during their many years of marriage.

Sometimes the need for affection is buried under a compensatory demand—not the exclusive attribute of the old, I would like to add. The attention seeker lists his wants: a drink, a newspaper, his pills, his window closed or opened. He wants something, anything, but what he really wants is for someone to care. The sad fact is that whiners and those who make excessive demands are avoided, while the compassionate, the supportive are themselves the recipients of affection and kindness. This is not a recent phenomenon; back in the fifth century St. Paulinus of Nola captured the relationship between helping and health. He said, "The needy are our healing."

Negative emotions are part of old age as they are at any other period of life. There are those for whom anger seems to be a way of life, whose emotional upheaval is evidenced by a snarl and a glare, whose short fuse leads to over-reaction, itself creating remorse. "I know I am not easy to live with," often follows an outburst.

Understanding the causes of anger, whether in ourselves or in others, can help in keeping it under control. Aging is exploring an unknown country. One has the map, but the reality of the terrain is different from the concept. The high and low areas have not been anticipated. It takes courage to change a lifetime, to alter relationships, to relinquish activities as they become impossible. It is exasperating not to be able to do normal things. When a concerned voice asks "Are you feeling all right?" even a simple answer becomes a problem. "Yes" is a lie when every breath is an effort. "No" sounds sullen when it is quite simply the truth one does not want to pursue. Sometimes anger means that the spirit has not given up.

According to T.S. Tsasz, people need familiar objects, familiar norms, familiar lifestyles, familiar friends. What can be more devastating than the loss of the familiar self? Anger is an uncomfortable, potentially dangerous emotion; obviously, getting upset doesn't help the blood pressure, and anger increases frustration to the point of illness. Pushed to the ultimate by it, two people who once loved each other dearly can turn to violence.

It is clear that when a situation cannot be changed the best one can do is to hang loose. And yet, pointing that out, insisting that an irritation is minor, can be a fresh irritant. I remember explaining an annoying situation as "such a petty thing."

"Exactly," a friend agreed. "So why are you making such an issue of it?"

I shared this reaction with a peer who was not as easily

"conned" as I had been. "That's easy enough to say," she objected. "But small things can take on a terrible dimension. When transportation is a problem the fact that the cobbler forgot your shoes is no minor issue. I can stub my toe against a rock, but it is the pebble in my shoe that raises the blister."

So, we have to recognize that to be angry is not always a bad thing. Some situations demand such a response at any age. Last week I had a phone call from an irate woman who had just been told by the administrator of a group-living unit, "Your mother just expired. Will you contact the undertaker or shall we?" That the young woman was angry and in shock as a result of the insensitivity is to be understood, and that she expressed her feelings was admirable, since it may save another family a similar experience.

In situations when the admonition to "be angry and sin not" is the crux of the problem, we may be encouraged by remembering that Jesus, who accepted the passion, who made no answer to Herod who mocked him, responded to the blow of the servant of the high priest with: "If I spoke evil, give testimony of the evil, and if not, why did you strike me?"

An elderly friend recovering from a stroke told me the difficulties she was experiencing as the last doorways to her independence slam shut. "Even when they appear to offer me a personal choice it isn't," she said. "It is 'Would you like to wash up?' and the unspoken order is '*Now*.'"

I was told of a volunteer worker who was asked to give up her job because a younger person was wanted. "White hair projects the wrong image," she was told. Too angry to even quote the anti-discrimination law, she wonders whether, since it was a volunteer, no-salary position, the law was applicable. Ironically, her younger substitute did receive a salary for the same work. For the older woman not to have been resentful would have been to accept an injustice.

Some anger, psychologists tell us, is actually fear, a response to a perceived threat, and as such is certainly justified. An older person living in a high crime neighborhood has a rational basis for fear and apprehension. Several commonly used drugs, both prescription and "over the counter," can cause anxiety in susceptible patients. "They didn't tell me what the side-effects might be," wailed an elderly woman in whom a chemical imbalance had hospitalized her with symptoms of depression. Some psychologists equate depression with anger against self which complicates the issue even more. Statistics reveal a frightening increase in suicide by the elderly, especially among men.

But the final years are not a barren time for everyone, nor are all days dark for anyone. For many the end of life is lived with a sudden recognition of the God who brings comfort, light, relief and healing to his own. Rahner, at the end of his long, productive life, held that old age gave the chance to sum up one's entire life, to get oneself together before the final mystery.

This is not to say that John Wood, of the Center for Studies of the Person in La Jolla, California, is not right when he calls attention to the silly platitudes with which the elderly are bombarded. "Don't let yourself get angry; it doesn't do any good. Don't cry. Things will be all right"— lip-comfort so obviously false the realization should stop the speaker mid-sentence.

The quick, emotional response of age has been labeled "the too easy tears of the old." I wonder why "too easy." Might it be that for many Americans the soft element of sympathy has hardened? Is teaching children not to cry, to close off emotions, as praiseworthy as it is pictured? We responded negatively to Archie Bunker's "Edith, stifle yourself," but the insistence that "big boys don't cry" is equally a denial of our essential humanity, and an expression of the fear that our peers may think less of us. The evangelists did not think Christ was weakened by the tears over Jerusalem, or at the grave of Lazarus. In him, and in us, a healthy expression of emotion is a positive.

Even in this society that does not honor feelings, being afraid, sadness, and anxiety, as well as love, compassion and gentleness, are human qualities. To tell one in pain, whether mental or physical, that life itself is a glorious gift is being insensitive to the fear. No one should be ashamed of being human.

Emotions need not rule our lives, nor do they. We can rest in faith regardless of the winter years. We can wish we were stronger at the same time that we delight in the powers we still have. We taste experience with delight as a special gift from God who does not forget us, who "neither slumbers nor sleeps." St. Paul summed it all up, "Nothing can separate us from the love of God."

When the Feeble Senses Fail

The Greek philosopher Aristotle, several centuries before Christ, noted that all learning comes to us through the senses. We in this century and this country have had dramatic evidence of the truth of this statement in the life of author and lecturer Helen Keller, blind and deaf from infancy. The world was closed to her until her teacher unlocked the doors to communicating to the gifted child through the sense of touch. While medical science has indicated that there are literally hundreds of bodily senses through which the human mind experiences the world both outside and inside the body, for most of us the five familiar senses of sight, hearing, smell, taste and touch come to mind when we hear the word.

The loss of any single sense can be devastating; fortunately, for most people, increasing years bring diminishment, but not total loss. However, failing eyesight, blurred sound, lowered taste perceptions, and decreased ability to handle and distinguish lowered temperatures and weights become a seriously limiting accompaniment to age. As with other aspects of growing old, the acuity of the senses fades so gradually that often one is not aware of the problem until some accident or crisis forces recognition.

In early middle age one jokes about arms not being long enough to read the telephone book. Gradually we notice that newspapers and magazines are using smaller type, that colors are more muted, and street lights have a foggy aura. Increasing age has decreased the ability of the eye to change shape and thus to focus on very near objects. It is true that a large proportion of older people compensate for poor focusing ability with glasses. But the eye of the average sixty year old admits only one-third as much light as the eye of the average twenty year old, which means that greater levels of illumination are required of us older people.

Because driving a car is a task where visual sharpness is especially important, it represents a good way to illustrate the physical effects of aging on sight. With corrected vision by age sixty more than ninety percent of people are still visually eligible for unrestricted driving, and, surprisingly, at eighty, seven out of ten are still visually eligible, with another fifteen percent visually eligible for daytime only driving. This, of course, does not mean rush-hour maneuvering on the Los Angeles Freeway, but it does indicate that with compensating mechanisms, such as corrective lenses, hearing aids, and medication when needed, a level of functioning required of a typical adult can be maintained longer than is usually believed. This is important, for the ability to be mobile guarantees independence and a healthy outlook on life.

Older people seem to adapt to darkness about as fast as the young, but their level of adaption is not nearly so good. This poor adaption to darkness can cause problems with night driving, as those of us who drive recognize; we do exercise extra care when driving at night. One positive in this litany of negatives in sensory loss is that we see signals as well; it is much easier for us oldies to distinguish yellow, orange and red than darker colors.

For most older citizens, to drive or not to drive is one of the easier decisions in this period of declining vision. A greater concern is the difficulty in reading instructions on food packages or on medication containers. There is also increased concern over potential blindness from macular degeneration, glaucoma or cataracts. Only about twenty-five percent of those over seventy have cataracts, that condition in which clouding of the eye's lens diffuses light, heightens sensitivity to glare, occasionally produces pain when the eye is exposed to even moderate light, and impairs vision. But statistics have little to do with a heightened awareness of the personal possibility. We fear the eventuality of seriously impaired vision and the traumatic adjustments it entails. It would be another kind of blindness not to recognize the possibility of serious vision loss as the years pile up.

A blind friend who has come to terms with his disability described its onset quietly. "There has been blindness in my family; these things go in families, they say. But at first I thought little of it. It was a cloudiness initially, and it came and went. We think that a blind man lives in eternal night, but it is not like that at all. It is as though someone flung a pan of milk into your face. I can tell the daylight from the dark, and in the daylight I can make out forms and shapes. There is this curtain between them and me, and for the first year or so I wanted to tear the curtain."

Preparing for blindness is not easy. The young can learn braille, but it is difficult for older people whose sensitivity of touch has also become impaired. Radio, TV, and books on tape can take the place of the printed word, but the visually impaired must learn to cope with unfamiliar territory, to feel for the food on the plate, to restrict movement lest a glass be upset, with the embarrassment which follows. Recently I had an opportunity to note how differently society reacts to such an accident when it is an awkward young person involved, rather than an elderly sight-impaired individual. I was having lunch with relatives in a restaurant when the charming waitress reached to remove a plate, and in so doing upset the tumbler of water. A tumbler holds a surprising amount of fluid, we all discovered, as it flowed over me and the table. I insisted that it was only water and no harm was done; my table companions used napkins to wipe up the spreading pool, emphasizing that it was a no-fault accident. "It could happen to anyone."

What we said and did was correct, of course, but I have also witnessed a similar upset occasioned by a legally blind woman. The cleaning up was equally efficient, but there was not the same emphatic reassurance, just a silent sopping-up exercise, a replacing of the spilled glass with a patient, "There, that's all right now," as a kind of concluding pat on the head. Probably the spilled glass in that case was a more frequent occurrence, but I am sure it is a painful embarrassment each time—a reminder that blindness has little by little robbed her of control. What a formidable thought for anyone.

I sat at table for some time with a sight-impaired friend, and watched her prepare for each accident-free meal with scrupulous care, placing each dish in a precise pattern grown familiar through routine. Not until every saucer, plate, glass and piece of silverware was precisely in position did she risk the hazardous venture of eating. If this seems exaggerated, I suggest that the reader go blindfolded to dinner and see how difficult the simple becomes.

The characteristic shuffle of the recently blind is born of a justifiable fear of tripping over unseen objects, of falling and breaking bones. A report in the *Journal of the American Geriatric Society* indicates that approximately 40,000 of the 150,000 Americans who suffer from hip fractures each year are believed to have fallen due to poor vision. A reluctance to be a bother frequently leads to withdrawal, isolation and depression in the blind, and there is documentary evidence, notes ophthalmologist Robert A. Soucher, that there have been false diagnoses of senility. It is impossible for those of us who have sight, and take seeing for granted, to comprehend the restrictions that low visibility places on normal life functions, especially for the elderly who are dealing with additional physical handicaps.

Recently I saw the demonstration of a cane with radar attachment which will enable the blind to detect objects and determine their relative position—a kind of inanimate seeing-eye dog; a beeper goes off should the cane be dropped, enabling the owner to retrieve it. But so far as I know the device has not yet been marketed, and when it is, I wonder about its price tag.

Years ago a popular if sentimental novel described a young woman wearing bandages in order to relater to her husband who had been blinded in war. While not very practical it hints at an empathy most of us do not have. I have seen occupational therapy students spend days in wheelchairs, with walkers, on crutches, wearing blinders to acquaint them with the problems of those they hope to help. But even they admit it does not approximate the reality, for they know the restrictions are only temporary.

For those with failing sight it is essential that they try to come to terms with the incomprehensibility of the situation by an increased personal relationship with God. In the Old Testament there is only one recorded cure from blindness, that of Tobias by the Archangel Raphael. But in the New Testament it is obvious that Christ was especially aware of the problems of the blind, and his compassionate outreaching to them is recorded repeatedly in the gospels. St. Matthew reports such healings twice, both times of two blind men traveling together who cried, "Lord, Son of David, have mercy on us." Exegetes debate whether this was actually one or two healings, but for us the importance of the story is the tenderness of Jesus, who in both instances, "moved with pity, touched their eyes." In St. Mark's gospel the blind man is not anonymous; he is Bartimaeus, son of Timaeus. He also cries out, "son of

David, have pity on me," and so does the blind beggar of Jericho in St. Luke's gospel. St. Mark tells of another blind man of Bethsaida whom Jesus took by the hand. For St. John the cure of the blind man is an opportunity for a number of catechetical lessons, but through the long narrative the relationship of Jesus with the blind beggar is never forgotten.

These are the only recorded cures of the blind, but one is justified in believing that there were more, since Jesus placed special importance on them in his answer to St. John the Baptist's disciples who asked whether he was the messiah: "The blind see, the deaf hear...the poor have the good news preached to them."

The elderly sight-impaired can take heart from this clear concern of the Lord who is still with us, and very close to them. While they cannot expect a cure in the literal sense, there is a spiritual blindness which for Jesus was more destructive of the person than physical blindness. All of us are weakened by this inability to see to some degree, and the cry of the blind man can effect a cure: "Jesus, Son of David, have mercy on me. Lord, that I may see."

Meister Eckhart said, "Truly it is in the darkness that one finds the light." Fr. Carrotti adds a contemporary note when he says, "In the darkness I feel that I must search. I shall search in him, now that I have begun to know him by living experience." And the blind frequently do have this extra sensitivity, a sight that penetrates what would otherwise be impenetrable darkness of the soul.

I recall some years ago when a sister with whom I lived lost her sight after unsuccessful surgery. Her quiet response to the doctor who gave her the devastating news was, "God gave me sight for the other sixty years; I can give it back to him freely now, and live with the memory of the beauty he allowed me to see."

Recently I was asked whether I would prefer to be blind

or deaf. My response was, I think, a normal one: "I would prefer neither." But I have given some thought to the question since, and my conclusions have made me more conscious of the problems of those with whom I live for whom sounds have become dim, as well as for those for whom the world is blurred. Actually, most of us, I suspect, think that being shut off from the beauty of the changing seasons or the loveliness of loved ones' faces would be the greatest loss. But in our oral society I wonder whether the deaf may not experience the greater deprivation.

Hearing loss causes social problems; it becomes more difficult to meet people, to partake of and enjoy group gatherings, to be a participant in a discussion, or even to enjoy a joke. More than ten million Americans have some hearing loss, and almost thirteen percent of the older population is deaf or severely hard of hearing, and consequently deprived of these simple social activities.

Communication becomes a major problem, since poor hearing makes it difficult not only to receive messages, but to send them. As a result older people with hearing loss tend to withdraw from conversation, commenting only when they are fairly sure they have heard correctly. Since for most of us the auditory impulses are received automatically, we find it difficult to understand the strain of continual concentration required of those for whom lip-reading, body language, facial expression, and gestures, linked with intelligent guessing, are substitutes for sound.

Last fall I signed up for a series of lip-reading classes. I planned to be prepared for the day when it would be a needed skill. I learned many things, but probably the most appalling, as well as the most surprising, was that lip-reading is guess-work about ninety percent of the time. So many sounds look alike—p, b, and m, for example; w and wh; ch and j; sh and g; s and z; t and d; n and l. Try distinguishing, as you look in the mirror, the difference that is visible as you say the words man, ban, pan. Add to the problem for the speech reader the fact that many people mumble. Turn down the sound on the TV and see how much of the speech you can understand, even when the speaker is facing full front. This illustrates slightly the problem that the hearing-impaired experience, and if, as is the case with many of the elderly, diminished vision is added, the difficulties are compounded. An interesting, and not totally irrelevant, fact is that while in ordinary conversation the hard of hearing find that the lower pitched male voice comes through more clearly, for the lip-reader the woman who uses lipstick is more easily understood, since her mouth defines sounds more distinctly.

Not hearing conversations makes one anxious about misinterpreting and reluctant to participate in discussion, and this leads to isolation. Who can blame the individual who feels out of touch, since that is actually the case.

There are procedures that both those with hearing loss and those communicating with them can follow to ensure that the bridge of silence is spanned. For the hard of hearing these tips include asking the speaker to repeat, to rephrase, to shorten, to spell. For those communicating with one with a hearing problem it is essential to speak slowly and clearly, to face the individual, to ask for confirmation to assure that what has been said has been understood. All too frequently the hearing partner repeats with obvious annoyance, and the hearing-impaired react by deciding that conversation isn't worth the struggle. With all these roadblocks to what is automatic give and take for most of us, it is not to be wondered that the elderly tend to disappear even from a family gathering, or to slip quietly into the background.

It need not be, of course, but overcoming the handicaps needs constant awareness on both sides. I recall my first experience with a totally deaf person and my amazement at her control of the situation. I was a young nun, recovering from surgery, when an elderly woman was brought into the room next to me—one of those double rooms with curtain between. After the IV's and oxygen had been activated, the orderly brought a child's slate and chalk, and attached it to the bed frame. The patient's communication with doctors, nurses and therapists was simple; she talked, they wrote. Even with the many electronic aids available today, writing is still a simple and sure means of making sure one is understood, and of breaking down the silence barrier.

There is signing, of course, but, for the elderly, it, like Braille, is an impractical solution. It is difficult to learn, and useless in most situations, for unless the one with whom you are signing also understands, it communicates nothing. While hearing loss cannot be cured, most hearing-impaired do surprisingly well with electronic help. Until the 1920s those with what is today considered a moderate hearing loss were considered deaf because so little help was available. The first electric hearing aids were developed at the beginning of the century and revolutionized the help available for those who face the difficult auditory demands of everyday life: the knock at the door, the cry for assistance, telephone, smoke or burglar alarms. Emergency warning devices and wake-up alarms, as well as telephone and doorbell signalers, use a transmitter and a receiver which plugs into an electrical outlet. Most of these use flashing lights similar to the message phone in hotels. Gadgets for the TV cue into coding for the hearing-impaired, and soon all TV's made in the United States will be equipped with closed-circuit captions for the hearing-impaired. Because of the "Americans with Disabilities Act," most hotels now have special devices available for guests with hearing loss.

But for many of the elderly living on a fixed income, these aids are financially prohibitive. Even hearing aids can be expensive, since the reputable ones, together with the doctor and audiologist fee, can cost more than four figures. However, if one is to continue to move freely outside the home, and even for communication within it, hearing aids, like spectacles, are a necessity, not a luxury.

An interesting article in the April 30, 1992 issue of *Science* reports on an experiment conducted in Liège, Belgium, by which damaged hair cells in the inner ear were regenerated with a vitamin A derivative similar to that used in the wrinkle cream Retin-A. The article warns that curing hearing loss in humans is years away, but since damage to the hair cells has been thought to be permanent, this is exciting news.

But until this or other cures are available, the deaf will continue to live in their silence. For some elderly, however, the deafness is not even silence. They are plagued with a continual ringing in the ear, sometimes comparatively soft, sometimes like rushing water. It is not wonder that they show signs of irritability; their nervous system is under continual barrage. Dr. Dean Ornish contends that being isolated is the greatest tragedy for a human being, and the most generic form of stress. Add to this the intrusion of unwanted sound, and the problem is compounded.

The wonder is that the sensory-impaired around us are for the most part so serene, so accepting, so adept at finding productive things to do. Beethoven continued to compose symphonies after he became deaf, musical marvels he himself never heard except mentally. One of my hard-of-hearing friends does not compose music, but she hears it internally. She loves to sit quietly with a musical score before her, and as her eye wanders over the notes her memory recreates the music she once enjoyed. I shared this with a couple of retired deaf friends, and they took to it enthusiastically, if less classically. They told me they now sing silently songs they knew when they were young.

Fortunately reading is still a possibility, as are crafts, and for many there is real satisfaction in creating.

What about the aged who are both blind and deaf? How do they cope? As with all disabilities, each handles it in an individual way. I live with a legally blind sister who says, smilingly, "I don't hear so well." That is an understatement, for she responds only when gently touched. But she is always in control and always interested. Frequently she asks, "How is the president doing?" She is not, so far as I know, a dedicated Democrat; her interest and concern are for the man holding the frightening office, and she wishes him well. One can hear her humming songs from her childhood in the hallways. I overheard her telling a companion, "We have to make our own happiness." And she does.

Many transcend their isolation by connecting with the center of love and strength, in what is a visible prayer life. One sister told me that she no longer thinks about the way things were, but enjoys imagining the way things will be, for "eye has not seen, ear has not heard, nor has it entered into the heart of man to conceive what things God has prepared for those who love him."

We do not generally think of the failure of the senses of taste and smell as very important, but doctors tell us that we are wrong. While we do not have the delicate sense of smell that animals possess, we do depend on what we have more than we are usually aware. Diminishment has even meant death for some who did not smell gas in their homes, or the smoke that signaled fire.

A recent British study indicates that the loss of the sense of smell can be a health hazard if not recognized. Doctors doing the study noted that malnutrition in the elderly was often linked to the loss of smell. Since taste and smell are strongly linked (try tasting a variety of soups with the nose blocked) some aromas are necessary for the detection of a distinct flavor. We link coffee, bacon and eggs, and popcorn with their fragrances. Functional changes in both nose and tongue, associated with increasing age, result in the loss of both taste and smell. As a result the elderly tend to eat less than they need.

Flavor is a key factor in palatability, and has a good deal to do with satisfaction. The British study indicates that all four qualities—sweet, salt, bitter, and sour—show an increase in threshold after age fifty. While the loss of taste and smell is not usually life-threatening, poor appetite resulting in poor nutrition can be. One resident of a retirement home commented with wry humor that since there was a removal of salt for those with heart problems, of fat for those with high cholesterol, and of sugar to accommodate those with diabetes, and the meat is ground for those with denture problems, the best that can be said for the meals is that they are nourishing.

Substitute satisfactions are available, but as someone remarked about an ad demonstrating that cereal was sugar-free and fat-free and "we are care-free": "Freedom is not all it's cracked up to be!"

The international food industry is slowly awakening both to the graying population, and to the challenge of maintaining sensory enjoyment of food as we age. The use of herbs can give savor to otherwise bland foods and help maintain the intensity of sensory stimulation. But in the last analysis pleasure in eating, so essential for physical well-being, is one more loss that the elderly experience.

I mentioned this recently to a young woman whose response startled me. "Eating is gross, anyway," she said. I thought of how often food and drink figure prominently in the gospel: Christ's first miracle of the changing of water into wine for the pleasure of guests who had already shared the groom's limited supply of inferior vintage; the multiplication of the loaves and fishes for the five thousand; Jesus' suggestion that the little daughter of Jairus be given something to eat. He ate with his friends, with Simon the Leper, with Zacchaeus, with Mary, Martha and Lazarus, and with the twelve at the last supper. Even after the resurrection there is a homely humanity about the offering to eat of the fish and honeycomb in the upper room, his evening meal and the breaking of bread with the two disciples at Emmaus, his preparing the breakfast at the seaside for his fishing apostles, and his invitation for them to contribute of their own catch. How often, too, the kingdom of heaven is portrayed as a banquet. It is intriguing to recall that Jesus told the disciples that he would not drink of the fruit of the vine until he drank it with them again in heaven.

And, them, there is the wonder of all wonders "My flesh is bread indeed, my blood is drink indeed. Take. Do this in memory of me." And we call it thanksgiving, eucharist. Clearly, God who gave us appetites does not consider them gross.

In all this reflecting on sensory deprivation of the elderly there is one important issue—we must recognize the common character of their loss, and acknowledge that in greater or lesser degree, we have deep similarities. Karl Rahner called attention to our own sensory lacks. We do not see infra-red; we do not hear the acoustic waves which a bat uses with its "radar"; we have no direct receptive organ for radio waves. Angelus Silesius noted: "The senses are in the spirit all one sense and act; he who sees God tastes, feels, smells and hears him, too." In him we live and move and have our being, and in him we learn to see.

When Power Diminishes

When Justice Thurgood Marshall retired from the Supreme Court in 1991 a brash young reporter asked him, "What's wrong with you?"

"What's wrong with me?" he answered. "I'm old and coming apart." That succinct statement summarizes the condition of many who find that their bodies no longer serve them uncomplainingly. The ordinary business of living is no longer ordinary; its most casual activities demand planning, concentration, effort and care. From waking in the morning until the final pulling up of the covers at night, the day is a careful handling of details, which to those of fewer years are automatic. If there is no pain on awakening it is cause for thanks to God for the gift. There are, of course, those who praise him even in pain, like the Irishman who, in response to those who asked how he was feeling, invariably answered, "Poorly, thanks be to God."

For many, just getting out of bed can cause dizziness from sudden change of blood pressure; moving must be approached by degrees. Bending to put on shoes is a similar risk procedure, so loafers or pumps into which the feet can be slipped are preferred to shoes which require tying. Arthritis restricts movements, requiring simple clothing with front closures, and large armholes. Decreased grip and joint mobility makes buttons difficult to manipulate, and Velcro is almost a must. Since wearing attractive clothes is a means of self-expression, it is important that control of personal appearance be maintained through the use of simple clothing adaptations.

Dangers in our surroundings—irregularity in floors, curbs, or door thresholds—can compromise postural stability, but denial of physical limitations is equally hazardous, so the early morning walk to the bathroom must be handled with discretion.

Since medications are important in controlling physical problems it is important to set up an inflexible schedule, in itself a bit of a poser. Medications to be taken once or twice a day are easy—they can be disposed of early and forgotten. But the three-times-a-day or every-four-hours pill requires reminders. Even the young tend to forget them. Some medicines have short-term side-effects visible to an observer, such as respiratory inhalants which may produce tremors (and embarrassment) and diuretics, essential for those with cardiac or pulmonary difficulties, which make one reluctant to leave the convenience of home.

Levels of chemical absorption are very personal, and doctors carefully calibrate dosage to the individual patient, so that adhering to the schedule is essential to maintaining stable health. I have found that taking those medicines which are one-a-day in the morning when I brush my teeth (if the medicine can be absorbed on an empty stomach) disposes of them at once. Those which need food can be taken immediately after breakfast, and the rest linked to a regularly occurring activity. I became aware of the importance of timing a year ago when I was having cardiac insufficiency in spite of wearing a Nitro-patch. I was hospitalized, monitored, and tested, after which the cardiologist did not change the prescriptions, just the hour for administration to fit the body's changing waxing and waning needs. Regularity, I discovered, is very important, and the exact following of time is curative.

There are a number of aids to memory on the market, even a beeping pill box, but for most of us a schedule rigidly adhered to will do the job.

Another difficulty for the elderly with weakened grip and muscle control can be the containers themselves. We have seen the cartoons and heard jokes about the child-resistant medicine caps which no one but a child can open. For the frustrated older person who desperately needs the medicine and does not have the coordination to "line up arrows and push," it is not a joke.

Breakfast itself, indeed eating in general, is no longer a pleasant diversion; hands crippled with arthritis do not grasp knife and fork with ease. There are special forks, knives and spoons with large handles, but unless one is regularly and seriously handicapped, they do not appeal, for they are conspicuous.

Buttering a piece of toast can be a major enterprise, and spooning a grapefruit is so out of the question that fruit juices become the automatic choice. But juices can be a balancing challenge and coffee cups a trick. One aging friend told his wife he finally understood why his grandfather always drank his tea from a saucer—it was easier. The crash of dropped dishes is not so frequent now that plastic dishes are available and in very attractive patterns. They are acceptable as part of the ordinary table setting, but TV trays carry a subtle insult. I heard one older citizen remark with disdain, "They remind me of dog dishes."

With breakfast over, our older, physically restricted friend now has a whole beautiful day to devote to whatever activities attract. And that is the problem. Most activities are out of bounds, since they require physical competence one no longer has.

Neurological or orthopedic problems may make mobility impossible, other than with a cane or walker, or even in a wheelchair—restraints an otherwise vital personality finds irksome. Getting about is so common for most of us that we never give it a thought until something turns up which restricts the use of our legs. For most of our lives we seek out our environment, change it at will, moving from place to place with scarcely a thought. Now at the end we need assistance, and these artificial means can be cause for gratitude. Recently I had a call from a retired friend in Arizona who had phoned to share with me her sense of freedom with the new collapsible walker she had acquired which opened up for her fresh avenues of independent living.

There are many self-help devices available for a more controlled lifestyle, and they should not be scorned; rolling carts, flashlights with long pressure bars, padded pot holders, long-handled dust pans and shoe horns, magnifiers with light attachments, some of which can be fitted to the book, magnifying mirrors for grooming, raised toilet seats, hand-held showers with extension hose, and my favorite gadget—the long-handled tweezers which enables me to pick up anything without bending.

All this brings us to a crucial consideration: we hate being propelled by things out of our control, the physical and mental precariousness that comes from being on the edge of incompetence. Reactions to such vulnerability range from anger to apathy, from pain to depression, but scarcely anyone is pleased at the prospect. What makes the position especially difficult is that dependent people are supposed to give up the right to lead their own lives. Most of us who have spent a half-century or more as independent adults rebel at the idea of assuming this position, and rightly so. There are independent, vigorous elderly persons with a long list of serious illnesses who are functioning all around us. There was a James Brown song that might well be our theme song, "I don't want nobody to give me nothing; just open up the door and I'll get it myself."

One of the outstanding problems faced by the elderly is boredom in the long day that stretches before them, a lack of stimulating possibilities available to those with handicaps of whatever nature. Walking, experts tell us, is the ideal exercise, and it can be an occasion for seeing and hearing the creation around us, of becoming more aware of nature's capacity to mirror not only the beauty but the mystery of God. Enjoyment of surroundings can be a prayer of experienced gratitude and wonder. Keeping a journal of the special experiences of each day—the explosion of magnolia blossoms, the rhythm of young willow branches in the spring wind, a dew-heavy spider web, a child's delighted laughter—can be effective in re-creating the experience at some future date. A friend and I recently spent a happy half hour listing shades of the colors viewed from our window, more shades than either of us had vocabulary to cover. Sometimes simply observing is a way to wonder. A little girl visiting with her parents pointed to a rainbow which her elders had not noticed, and cried, "See, God still loves us." When I heard her I thought of how often we adults see a rainbow, remark on its fragile beauty, and forget what the little girl remembered, that it is a sign of God's covenant with us, as well as an atmospheric phenomenon.

But for some with unstable angina, ventricular arrhythmia or exercise-induced asthma, admirable though it be, real walking is contraindicated. The Penn State Sports Newsletter recently reported that more than ten percent of Americans are affected to some degree by these conditions, whose symptoms include shortness of breath, coughing, gripping, tight or burning sensations in the chest, and incapacitating fatigue. The number of such persons increases and pulmonary function decreases with age. So, if we are so afflicted, we look for other things than walking to fill the hours.

Raising plants, even nursing an ivy in a small pot when space is a deterrent, can help us stay close to the miracle of life itself. Even the simple planting of an orange or lemon seed that we did with our children years ago can be satisfying now as we watch the small blade pierce the soil and expand its territory. It isn't gardening, but in the smaller parameters of age, it is a surprisingly satisfactory substitute. Any increased knowledge and the resultant excitement can make a difference in reasons for getting out of bed each day, and will help us enjoy each one a little more.

Doctors Abrams and Barkow, who have done extensive studies of the aging, believe that while general slowing down is typical, when the old are allowed to work at their own speed, new skills, new knowledge, new ideas, new points of view are easily acquired. In their words, "the elderly are flexible, resourceful, optimistic."

Cardinal Newman is said to have taught himself a new language every five years, well into his eighties, repeating phrases while he shaved. And that was in the nineteenth century before there were tape-recorded aids to language learning.

Some years ago I was introduced to an elderly Franciscan who, I had been told, was a linguist. I presumed that with that title he probably knew Latin and Greek, perhaps French, German or Spanish. When I asked how many languages he knew he said, "It depends upon what you mean. I read about two dozen, speak another dozen, and understand possibly a third dozen." When I looked my surprise he said, "Actually, it is easy, since languages fall into families. Once you have the basics you just keep adding vocabulary. Romance, Teutonic, Slavic, for the western world, and then the Oriental and African languages, each different, each basically the same. I never read English anymore," he continued. "I subscribe to foreign newspapers and magazines, and they keep me up to the mark." That was important, he added, for "I would never turn away anyone wanting to confess in one of thirty languages."

Most of us, I suspect, do not have his language aptitude, but if we have knowledge of any language other than English it is satisfying to read the news in that tongue, and worth the price of the subscription in the lift it gives the spirit.

Some years ago I lived with a retired artist who, following the example of Monet, studied one of the beautiful natural sections of our campus all through the day. One summer she did a series of paintings of the same scene showing the dramatic changes which occurred as the light changed from morning to twilight. For the housebound, such a study, even if not painted, can be done from a window overlooking a street, a meadow, a playground. It is the sort of quiet contemplation which brings with it a peace and serenity that leads almost automatically to prayer.

Gerontologists recommend as a hedge against depression that the senior citizen be engaged in learning something new all the time. One retired doctor of my acquaintance has begun to study stocks and bonds, a baffling enterprise. When I asked whether he played the stock market he answered, "No, of course not. I can't afford it, but my wife and I have made a game of imaginative investing each morning, checking in the evening to see how we did."

Birdwatching demands just the qualities which the aging possess: patience, calm, and the interest and excitement engendered with each new recognition recorded. It is a hobby that requires little equipment, although a pair of binoculars are an advantage, as is the fact that this hobby can be pursued from a wheelchair, or on foot, alone or with a friend.

There are innumerable books on the market, or, if buying is out of the question, in the public library, which suggest things to do or make, complete with diagrams or illustrations. All of us carry memories of skills we intended to develop, but for which we never found time. Now can be the time. I recall an elderly woman who, in spite of arthritis, decided to learn to play the harp, "rather than wait," she said, "to learn it in heaven." Why not? We might even tackle the computer; kindergartners seem to use it with facility.

Genealogy is one of the more popular avocations of many today, and here we older people have an advantage, for we bring to the research a lived memory. But even we, I have learned, have regrets: we did not ask our elders when we were young. As a colleague said, "When we have grandparents, we don't care; when we care, we don't have grandparents." So, as keepers of the tradition today, we have something invaluable to contribute: information about unrecorded events that have happened over the years in families, workplaces, communities, and the nation. Recently at a meeting of a committee working on one facet of the celebration of the Milwaukee archdiocese's one hundred and fiftieth anniversary the young archivist remarked, "You all are making an invaluable contribution to our records." Time blurs the focus, but sometimes it is our cataract-clouded eyes which can sharpen it.

As the years accumulate, remembering becomes a greater part of our days, and planning a pattern of remembering and prayer can be a wonderfully healing, happy experience. Years ago I was introduced to it by an old nun. The plan is this: with one day covering a decade, allocate as many days to the exercise as your lived decades. Each day reflect on one decade, calling up the people, places, things, events, which made each a special gift of the creator. One need not express formal thanks for each experience, but as they are relived, loving gratitude will spring spontaneously. We have so much for which to be thankful to God, and as we touch each experience, each person, gently in memory, the age-old question "Why me, God?" takes on a different twist. Why should I have had so much joy, so much comfort, so much love, so much health, so many successes, so many friends, so many graces? All were gifts, and, thanks be to God, they are my past.

An adaptation of that enriching of the present by remembering times past might be to call to mind people who have helped us through life, and, yes, those we think we may have helped, touching each with affection and gratitude to God for what they have meant. We might even linger on those dear people whose presence today makes the gray days bright, asking that God continue to bless them and us.

The church and the world live in a situation of transition, and so do we. Our lives have become more complicated, and we ourselves, perhaps, have become more complicated. As Karl Rahner noted, we have only a limited amount of time, a limited capacity to work, a finite potential. There is a big difference between what we would like, what we want, and what, given the current situation, we can hope for or expect. Aging is a very personal phenomenon, and is neither predictably positive nor predictably negative, although while things are seldom all one way or the other, as the years cast shadows and the physical disabilities narrow the horizons, there may appear to be more shadow than light.

Teilhard de Chardin, whose writings show an unusual awareness of this aspect of life, stressed that at the first approach of the diminishments, we cannot hope to find God except by loathing what is coming upon us and doing our best to avoid it. He believed that the more we repel suffering with our whole heart and our whole strength, the more closely we cleave to the heart and action of God, without bitterness and without revolt, but with an anticipatory tendency to acceptance and final resignation. "God must some way or other make room for himself."

This is a major task, and one for which most of us have had little preparation. We must learn to accept assistance from others without losing our self-respect. We must deal with society's growing resentment of its graying population. Just as blacks were long openly referred to as the white man's burden, the elderly are now openly proclaimed the young person's burden—belittled, excluded, pushed aside.

Bob Shanks in *Newsweek*, February 22, 1993, is specific as he writes about those who are eating up resources beyond their own usefulness. "90% of Americans," he says, "tell their pollsters that they believe in God and heaven, and yet you have to drag them, kicking and screaming, tubes dangling, to the Elysian elevator ascending to eternal bliss. Have they stopped believing in anything at all but their individual self-centered lives?" He continues with a number of proposals to deal with the problem, us. "Euthanasia will be added to the National Anthem, and the Pledge of Allegiance," and he urges us to "get off the stage and off the public weal."

The passage of a bill in Holland in 1993 making euthanasia an approved medical procedure, with conditions, of course, underscores the fact that Mr. Shanks was not being facetious. The subject is out in the open, and articles are proliferating which calculate the cost of keeping oldsters warehoused in nursing homes. All of this is the expansion of the expendable people principle, a "let's get rid of the deadwood" syndrome which, when applied to individuals, is harder to bear than the assault of years.

An increase in violent crimes against the elderly adds to the fear many live with, even in their own homes. As I write this today our local paper's lead story is of an eighty-nine year old woman attacked and robbed in her home twice in the past six weeks by neighborhood children, apparently led by a nine year old girl. Suffering from arthritis, the woman was beaten with her own cane, and her phone was ripped from the wall. The children, after ransacking the home, left with $30.

Asked by reporters whether she was scared, the woman replied laconically, "Who wouldn't be?"

It is no wonder that depression is growing among the elderly, with an estimated twenty percent of the older people so afflicted. According to Doctor Kra, an internationally recognized gerontologist of Yale University Medical College, the two major causes of depression in the elderly are the threat of lack of finances to eat or pay the rent, and its concomitant: dependence on others. People who have worked diligently all their lives with a certain degree of confidence and grace are now threatened with the loss of social security benefits, as well as increasing prices, rents and medical costs which can transform even the relatively secure elderly into terrified citizens. Faced with an illness that requires the purchase of expensive medications and other medical bills, depression sets in swiftly. And what of the elderly with little or no money, the poor?

And then there are the stereotypes to deal with. The fallacy of these is especially difficult to expose. In many cases, it is feared, the elderly role-play the part and become the non-person expected.

What a comfort it is that God, who scheduled aging in his creation of that marvelous complex mechanism, the human body, accepts us at every moment. For him advancing years are no matter for rejection. As Carrotti expresses it. "God offers the solution to all problems, the response to all darkness, often the blackest, and the smoothing away of all anxiety." He is the one to whom we can entrust ourselves; he is the vital support at this time of our lives, as he has always been. He is security in insecurity, strength in our weakness. He himself is our future.

We can cope, then, even with the realization that we are merely marking time, because in him our end is definitely our beginning. We can let go in total abandonment, in the dark, because we have heard his voice through Isaiah, "Courage. Do not be afraid. Look, your God is coming." It is in him that we make our peace with our mortality.

When Pain Is Ever-Present

This chapter will be brief, because the subject, pain, cannot be dealt with satisfactorily, if at all. Yet to omit it entirely, when it occupies so large a part of declining years, would be to avoid a truth. Although the philosopher Wittgenstein warns us to be silent concerning things we cannot speak about clearly, we need to acknowledge the reality of the human dimension in the body's agony.

Pain is always personal, and there are no words to describe it, even in the hospital where one is surrounded by others with similar symptoms. The definition the dictionary gives is so inadequate as to be ludicrous: an unpleasant sensation, occurring in various degrees of severity. To tell one in the breath-snatching vise of a severe angina attack that what is being experienced is an unpleasant sensation would be an insult. There are words that attempt to differentiate kinds of pain, and we recognize their validity; doctors use them as aids in diagnosis. A dull pain differs from a sharp one; a gnawing pain is as distant from stabbing as throbbing differs from steady. And yet, what do words say, really?

Many have felt the futility of measurement when asked to describe what they are suffering "on a scale of one to ten." What is number one in pain? What is ten? At the moment, this actual moment, all an individual can know is that a wave of pain has battered defenses and wiped out all other sensations.

The pain of childbirth, memorialized in scripture, is not

the only one, fortunately, that the sufferer forgets. Memory deposits only the fact that pain was. We can call up the picture of the house in which we grew up, the wooded lakeside where we camped, even the hospital room where we experienced pain. But we cannot, thank God, call up the pain. We remember that we had it, that it was disabling, that we dread its recurrence, but the actual experience of our own pain is as distant as if it were another's.

Before discussing various illnesses characteristic of the end of life, and the constant pain that so frequently accompanies them, I want to underscore the fact that the elderly do not have a monopoly on sickness, pain or death. There are thousands of children and young people who bear incurable diseases, whose days and long, sleepless nights are weighted with pain, and this chapter, indeed this book, is not indifferent to their suffering. But the theme of this book is aging, and the focus here is on those whose sicknesses are almost always the inevitable accompaniment of years, with the pain and the kind of "discrimination by disease" they bring. How one at that end of life deals with the situation differs from any other age. The young have reason to hope that a cure will be found; the old know that for them there is no cure. At this point, life's uncertainty opens to certain death.

In the absence of pain, sufferers from terminal disease can be remarkably light-hearted. Some time ago I was a visitor in an oncology hospice, and came upon a group of patients who were devastated by laughter. The reason for their amusement was a narration by one of their number of the ridiculous happenings she had experienced as a cancer patient: the embarrassed glances at her chemo-induced baldness when she lost her wig in a high wind; the problem she encountered shopping when barometric pressure loosened her prosthesis and she tried to wave down a taxi, her leg jutting from the crock of her arm. Her stories provoked a response from the others of ludicrous stories, a kind of black humor funny only to those who had suffered through similar incidents. There was a bond between these patients that I, cancer-free, could not share. They had found meaning in the absurdity and could relax in it.

Victor Frankl would have understood, for he had a significant message for all human beings, one especially applicable to the suffering elderly. "Man's concern is not to gain pleasure nor to avoid pain, but rather to see meaning in his life." That is why man is even ready to suffer on the condition that his suffering has a meaning. It is possible in the midst of pain to find meaning, to focus on being responsible to the situation, to use it as a means of greater freedom. But this must be done while one is in control. When pain strikes it takes over.

It is not that we become more selfish; it is, as anyone with experience recognizes, that pain centers the whole human organism on itself. Getting through the waves of anguish is the most the victim is capable of—and God does not ask anything more of us in that moment. Everything becomes unessential. It is not that those we love are not important, that our relationship to God has changed; it is just that when excruciating pain is there it envelops the total person.

It is not easy to talk to someone who is suffering; it may not even be the wisest thing to do. Silence and presence may be more appropriate, since they acknowledge the greater reality. Certainly the easy words of comfort, the well-worn platitudes serve no purpose. Presence, and a touch, a grasped hand, are more effective and more appreciated since they demand no response.

There is almost no organ in the human body that cannot be afflicted, and the list of diseases which afflict the aged with special force fill a huge medical tone. We are aware of the more common—cancer, stroke, emphysema, congestive heart failure, diabetes, osteoporosis, leukemia. William Osler referred to pneumonia as "the special enemy of old age," in the first edition of his famous textbook. In the third edition he called it "the friend of the aged." He died of it!

Physicians and patients deal with equally devastating, if less recognized, roots of pain: trigeminal neuralgia, hairline fractures, arteritis, intestinal blocks, myasthenia gravis, and a score of others. Recently a dear friend was diagnosed as having Shy Drager syndrome, a new disease of which I had never heard. It has no known cure. She faces four to six years, a long, slow ride to the grave, entombed within an unresponsive body: unable to move, speak or see, but, it appears, able to think. And this is but one of many. How often a newspaper account of a disease adds, "is most common in the elderly."

How often, too, we hear the comment, "Thank God, he didn't suffer long." Again, I am confronted by the question of time when it comes to pain, for pain is outside time. A moment is endless, an exploding now.

There are local chapters of the American Chronic Pain Association, a non-profit, self-help organization which helps chronic pain sufferers live more easily. Members are taught to manage and reduce pain's impact through stress reduction and relaxation techniques.

Human beings have always sought relief from pain. Archeological digs have discovered evidence that centuries ago men used some of the very analgesics now available in chemical combinations. The quality of life is very personal, and an elderly person with only a few months of life remaining should not have to spend them enervated by incessant nagging pain. So, reducing pain through the use of anodynes when possible is certainly justifiable. There is a problem with long-term chronic ailments, since medicines tend to lose potency when used over a period of time. Doctors aware of this and the probably urgent need for pain relief at a more critical terminal point tend to postpone the use of the more effective drugs.

Helping the body deal with pain is a body of chemicals in the brain called endorphins. They are ten times more powerful than morphine, and in addition the number seem to be increased in the elderly. But there are those who, for some reason or other, do not produce these self-initiated helps to dull the edge of suffering.

Doctors at both the University of Wisconsin and Boston's Dana Farber Cancer Institute have compared patients' pain levels and treatments with pain management guidelines drafted by the World Health Organization. According to the study twenty-five percent had pain severe enough to warrant treatment with more potent drugs; half the men and women over seventy, they discovered, were not getting the pain relief they needed.

The blame for this is not entirely that of attending physicians; patients are frequently reluctant to ask for relief. The elderly are especially hesitant to question a doctor's drug decision. And the "Just-say-no" to drugs movement has made both patients and doctors sometimes unduly concerned about the addictive potential in powerful pain killers. But certainly, one would think, at a time when life expectancy is predictably short, the problem of addiction as commonly understood is minimal.

A self-administered morphine pump is now available for those in intractable pain; the built-in limitations of dosage and timing make it safe for home use, and there is abundant evidence that the relief of pain aids the body in its own sedating, relaxing defense.

But inevitably we come back to the mystery of pain, the experiencing of evil in our own body. The mystery is there, and we cannot escape or avoid it. So, how do we deal with it? God can do anything, and if he wished he could stop the pain. He doesn't. We can go on arguing forever why God permits all suffering on earth. But what we actually know is that he alone has the answer. I believe it is Thomas Merton who reminds us that at baptism we were marked with the cross, and over the years we signed ourselves with it. Well, now, here it is!

But we do not have to be braver than Jesus in Gethsemane when, fearing what was to come, he prayed to be spared. There was no answer, at least none the gospel tells us, but he received the strength to go on and face the terrifying ordeal that awaited him. We, too, can hope that ultimately in some still unimaginable way everything will turn out to our good. And if we still find questions hiding within us, we can take comfort from Romano Guardini who, dealing with his own pain at the end of his life, said, "When I enter eternity I will ask how there can be so much suffering, pain, death and senselessness in the world."

Talk, then, is all very well, but pain when we feel it is another thing altogether. Both thought and prayer are beyond us when we are in its grip. We need to recognize now, pain-free at the moment, that living out this greatest of absurdities can be the deepest of prayers. This is the cloud of unknowing into which our single-word cry, "God," is hurled. Somehow at that most personal of moments we know that he has heard. We recognize that we are not bludgeoned by a blind, indifferent fate; we are carried by divine mercy, and somehow, somehow it will see us through.

When Forgetting Is Normal

Two sentences recur again and again in conversation with the elderly: "I don't want to be a burden," and "It doesn't matter what illness I get, if I just don't lose my mind." For most of us the fear of complete physical dependence and mental deterioration is greater than any other, and, sadly, both loom as distinct possibilities in our future. As a result, every slip of memory seems to be a warning forecast of the future.

We tell ourselves that everyone forgets; otherwise, why does our casual language include "Whoziz?" "Whatyacallit" and other similar linguistic cover-alls. For our comfort Dr. Stanford Finkel of Northwestern University Medical School notes that forgetfulness is more common in later life, but believes it is questionable whether or not it should even be considered an abnormality. Most individuals have not had to tax their memories after they finished their formal education. Everyone has a certain degree of absent-mindedness. Entering a room and forgetting the reason why one is there is a common enough occurrence. Society forgives the absent-minded professor for not remembering routine matters, since he is presumed to be preoccupied with profound thoughts, which may or may not be true. Then there are those who claim never to forget a face; they just can't remember the name. When a younger person returns from a shopping trip only to discover that he forgot to pick up the bread he laughs it off with a rueful, "I'd forget my head if it weren't screwed on." But the older shopper hides the forgetting, for fear of hearing, "His memory is slipping."

Information bombards the brain at every waking moment, and it requires attention to process it; many times we are alert but inattentive. However, the reality is that we cannot prevent aging, and general memory gaps do begin to appear, and since our memory bank defines who we are to some degree, it is distressing when it goes blank. We feel we have lost something of ourselves.

In spite of huge advances in medical knowledge of the way in which memory works, there is no quick, single test that determines whether our individual memory impairment is organic or a reversible problem. Gerontologists make every effort to find the cause, and, if possible, to treat it, but they are not always successful. When Cicero said, "I never heard of an old man forgetting where he has hidden his money," he was underscoring two truths: our tendency to cling to possessions, but also the fact that memory depends to a great extent on repetitive action and interest, and the ability to store material in the memory seems to be unaffected by age. Although things are processed more slowly, this has nothing to do with intelligence.

We senior citizens have learned to adjust. We establish a definite place for things we use frequently. Since the place always remains the same, the object and its location are reinforced in memory each time it is used. We have misplaced car keys too often, forgotten where we put our glasses, or that we had put water on to boil when the phone rang, interrupting the pattern. When rain has been predicted, we hang an umbrella on the doorknob to remind us to take it. We note a landmark every time we park a car, and some of us write it down. We work for association, and try to put things into categories. But in the "tip-of-the-tongue" experiences we don't strain. We know that memory is tricky, elusive, and will not be forced.

Dr. Robert Butler, chairman of geriatrics at Mt. Sinai School of Medicine in New York, suggests that we do not clutter our minds with trivialities; in any case, the longer we live, the more information we have stored, and that in itself makes retrieval more difficult. There is a mind-saving structure in the brain that acts as a clearing house for what is worth remembering.

Certainly intensity of attention and focus help memory retention, but that is not unique to old age. When I was a young woman in graduate school I decided not to take notes at lectures. If what I heard or read interested me I knew I would remember it. If it didn't, what I wrote would not mean much later. That system worked then, although I am not sure I would risk the method today, since I acknowledge that there is a memory deficit with the accumulation of years. We can take comfort, however, in the fact that it appears to be less for rote memory than for logical memory, and our retention of things heard becomes increasingly superior to the retention of things seen. The use of both, of course, gives better results than either does separately. But that, too, has a down-side; age is when sight and hearing loss occurs. For individuals shut as they are into a silent world, with little outside stimuli, there is little need to use memory, and the old jingle applies, "If you don't use it, you lose it." And so, some of us play games, because we have been told they can be a stimulus, especially word games such as Scrabble, crossword puzzles, even Trivial Pursuit. And we play increasingly complex card games that demand recall. One of my neighbors knows twelve different patterns for solitaire.

Dr. Bruckheim holds that while the type of memory that permits us to recall names may decline, important things do not disappear so readily. He has evidence which shows that even individuals in their seventies and eighties can often score as well on memory tests as many youngsters, and will remember material that has application to their daily lives. People who exercise their memories tend to maintain them well into old age, and some escape memory loss altogether. His conclusion is that most of us remain mentally self-sufficient throughout our lives.

But this generation knows about Alzheimer's and is frightened!

There are no blood tests, skin tests, or X-rays that can make a firm diagnosis of Alzheimer's, in spite of the fact that since 1974 the National Institute on Aging has been empowered to "conduct and support biochemical, social and behavioral research and training related to the aging process, and to disease and other special problems in the needs of the aged." My own congregation is a participating partner in such a study.

But for the elderly it is not academic or medical knowledge that has been acquired, but a collection of painfully gathered observations. We have had loved ones change from intelligent, competent, concerned individuals into vague, shuffling shadows of themselves. We have watched them lose the ability to handle ordinary tasks, lose interest in what is going on around them, lose the ability to make simple choices of what to wear and what to eat, and we have, in some instances, cared for them until we were no longer able. We have watched personality changes as a gentle, affectionate friend became violent and a self-assured one became agitated and frightened in a familiar world become strange. We have seen the massive confusion which the inability to organize one's small environment produces. We have dealt with the blank stare of non-recognition in a close relative, and the inhuman sounds of the human voice when speech is gone.

And knowing what we know, we ask ourselves if that is our future.

We know that the changes are very subtle, and initially barely noticeable: a loss of initiative, a decline in the ability to do familiar things, a certain apathy, difficulty with occupations that require manual dexterity such as playing the piano, typing, knitting, crocheting, even handling silverware.

It appears that most victims are aware of what is happening, and suffer this creeping disability in silence. They avoid conversation which requires recall and interpretation, and fabricate answers with stock phrases that fit almost any conversational gambit. I recall a friend who kept her condition hidden for some time with a collection of phrases: "You don't say. How interesting. I can't believe it. What an experience."

On the other hand, some, struggling with the realization that things are moving out of their control, talk incessantly, to anyone who will listen, of their fears, their frustrations, their anger. Afraid of everything, a feeling of having no life ahead, and of leaving nothing of value behind, they become a living demonstration of Robert Frost's hired man who had "nothing to look forward to with hope, and nothing to look backward on with pride." Telling them of their very real accomplishments makes no impression. Their answer is, "I've lived too long. I don't have anything."

I remember a gifted colleague saying desperately, "Something is wrong with my mind. I'm losing myself."

When such patients are finally forced to seek medical help, there is the long waiting, the humiliation of psychological testing, the sense that as objects of pity they are entering a prison from which there will be no escape, and in which they will serve their time. And we tell them to relax!

It is impossible for us who are not caught in this narrow, desolate reality to begin to understand their utter helplessness, the seeming endlessness of fear and depression.

Sometimes something happens to jolt us observers into realization and empathy. This winter I had such an experience, and difficult though it was at the time, I am grateful for the door to understanding it has opened.

A young friend and I were shopping together. I had a gift certificate which I intended to cash, so when she made a small purchase I gave the clerk the check and said, "I'll pay for that."

She ignored me, turned to my friend and said, "I can't cash this." She had equated my obviously senior status with an inability to deal with the simplest of financial matters, as she proceeded to explain to my companion, not to me, that she did not have enough cash to honor my request. I took back the check, and we moved on to a department where they were happy to deal with me, and to accept my money in spite of the snow on my roof. It is an uncomfortable experience, and I have often wondered whether those in the early stages of Alzheimer's, sensing doubt of their mental faculties in those around them, are as shattered by the realization as I was. I still do not understand the clerk's behavior, but it was a painful reminder that an insult can destroy human dignity. Given verbal and non-verbal messages of this nature, it is understandable that the recipients become ineffective.

So, while we elderly know that the disease of the century, Alzheimer's, affects only a small number, we do not know what lies ahead for us individually, and we wonder how we will be able to deal with the possible diminishments. We have seen that it can sometimes be a long journey of progressive suffering on many levels. When this thought becomes overwhelming our best comfort is the knowledge that this is the thing God has willed for us, and in it, strange as it may seem, his love is found.

Teilhard de Chardin recognized this. He wrote of the internal passivities that form the dark element in these desperate years. "Lying in wait for us, appearing as suddenly and brutally as an accident, or as stealthily as an illness.... Sometimes it is the cells of the body that rebel, or become diseased, at other times the very elements of our personality seem to be in conflict." But even then we do not want to explain away the unhappiness.

We do think of the future; we pray to him who said, "Let not your heart be troubled," for grace to live it; we also live in the present. Early literature on aging was full of assertions of a declining self-image. Recent studies, however, have shown that most older people do not have a negative self-image, and, in fact, that self-esteem tends to increase with age if its basis is not eroded. While biologically-based abilities do become less for all adults past fifty, there appears to be no loss in learning abilities.

The problem has been that tests designed and administered by relatively young researchers began with the premise that the younger subjects' values were the norm. Dr. Robert Butler, in *Aging and Mental Health*, points out that people of all ages, under pressure to perform more quickly than they can, will lose confidence, make mistakes, and become confused. These are symptoms of pressure, not of incompetence, not signs of deteriorating faculties. If given a bit more time, older people can usually learn anything, including computer analysis. Tasks that involve manipulation of concrete objects or symbols, distinct and unambiguous responses, and low interference from earlier learning are particularly liable to good performance by older people.

Dr. Alex Comfort of Stanford insists that the human brain does not shrink, wilt, perish or deteriorate with age.

It normally continues to function well enough through many decades. He believes that we could lose over half our brain cells and still have a billion more than we could ever need.

So, we have every reason to use whatever strategies are useful in keeping the mind active and the spirit buoyant. Among other things we should not be too credulous of what we hear or read about aging. Recently I had an example of how important this can be. In the doctor's waiting room I read in one of the magazines his receptionist had laid out that "those suffering cardiovascular diseases have lower intellectual performance." When I saw the doctor a few moments later I referred to what I had read, and his answer was an annoyed, "What fool wrote that nonsense?"

We can use the good time for the things we really want to do. A long-range project can be done if we tailor it to the energy we have. We may have to settle for what we can realistically undertake, and may have to refuse, reluctantly, what we cannot. St. Francis de Sales' "Refuse nothing, ask for nothing" may no longer be a viable way of life, but we do not need to stand by impotently and watch our world collapse.

And so, we manage to continue to live life quietly and normally. And yet—and yet... There is that appointment we forgot to keep, the bill we forgot to pay, the neighbor we did not recognize. Is this the beginning of the slow slide that we are powerless to prevent? There is no way that we can know.

In this time of doubt we try to accept the situation, putting our trust in God who has been with us throughout our life. Although he may not change the course on which our human nature is taking us, he will direct everything to the ultimate point of grace. Our short-term memory may be fading, but we have not forgotten the one who presides over and controls all the circumstances of our lives. And because there is not much time left there is an urgency to use it well. We learn to distinguish between what is important and what is not, to let go, even of ourselves, if that is what God wills. In his hands we know we are secure; he has promised that he will never forsake us. We may, if memory fails, forget him, but he will never forget us, and in that knowledge we are calm.

When We Leave the Familiar

A 1991 movie, *Fire in the Dark*, dealt with issues relative to care for the elderly, and the degree of responsibility of children to ensure it. The movie covered many of the bases: the widow whose husband died of a sudden heart attack, a fall resulting in a broken hip with a consequent lessening of independence, worries about the future, a slowly eroding capacity to deal with issues, forgetting, irritability, and rivalry between children which left the daughter to deal with the problem of her mother's decline. Together with this is the sub-plot of the erosion of the daughter's own family life, her husband's annoyance at the disruption of his home, and her son's resentment at his mother's apparent indifference to his needs. There is some wonderfully perceptive dialogue, as when the mother insists to a friend, "I'm going to die on my feet," and the friend's answer, "You don't have a choice."

It is all there, and I am sure movie-goers caught entirely different messages, depending upon their own age and experience. In fact, one reviewer sees Olympia Dukakis, the mother, as a woman who refuses to pay heed to her increasing infirmities. I, on the contrary, remember her desperate cry, "I'm so afraid; don't you see, I'm so afraid," as the issue. But whichever focus the script writer and director intended to stress, the movie does emphasize a reality.

Aging increases our sense of vulnerability; we become disabled and increasingly dependent. Older people dread being a burden, and when finances permit, they prefer retirement villages, group homes, Sun City, anything else. However, aside from the money involved, these are unrealistic alternatives for many. Just the problem of mobility is one deterrent. Even electric scooters, a real boon for those who have difficulty walking, either because of bone problems, or cardiac and lung disabilities, are not substitutes for good health. The advertisement which indicates that these provide independent living, with assembly so simple anyone can do it in minutes and store the chair in the trunk of a car, is not realistic. Those who use it are usually physically incapable of disassembling, lifting, and storing, and in many cases they do not drive. So, like Olympia Dukakis in the movie, they struggle.

Most people loathe the prospect of going into a nursing home, even the best. Although low income people would live much better than they ever lived, even they are reluctant. The question is: Why is this?

Robert Myers, chief actuary of the Social Service Administration, notes that they are mini-hospitals. People who are there have no alternatives. One social worker told me she wishes those who are considering arranging for a relative to enter one would themselves live in it for twenty-four hours before deciding. Recently I heard a comparatively young woman discussing her friend's dilemma. Her mother did not want to go into a home, and, commented the friend, "She is such a worry for Muriel." I knew the mother—elderly, yes, but completely competent, and gloriously independent. I measured her daughter's intermittent worry about her mother with that mother's restricted and limited life in an institution. The social worker was right—few people place themselves in the aging relative's position. There are, obviously, times when care becomes more than a family can cope with, but until that time comes it is always wise to wait.

A nurse friend asked me recently how this book was progressing, and I told her I was beginning the chapter on nursing homes. "Don't bad-mouth them," was her comment. "You may need one sooner than you think." A sobering thought.

My intention was never to write a collection of horror stories; the daily papers give us those. I do approach the topic from the point of view of one who, like countless others, faces the reality that there may be no alternative. Timothy Diamons, of the sociology department at California State University, wrote in 1992 a brave, compassionate study of the caretaking business, based on his own experience as a nursing assistant in several such homes. The book *Making Gray Gold* (University of Chicago Press, 1992) is probably one of the best contemporary studies of the bureaucracy of health care.

Until last year the whole subject of nursing homes was purely academic as far as I was concerned. We sisters had our own health care center, and that is where we expected to spend the end of our lives, and where we could eventually die. But with fewer young women entering the congregation, and a growing number of old and disabled with consequently less income, skilled care has become a financial and professional impossibility. We have, as a result, joined graying America as residents of nursing homes. Within the past ten months I have seen over a hundred of my peers leave for four nursing homes in Wisconsin, Illinois and Indiana. My visits to some of these have given me data, as have discussions with doctors and nurses.

There are currently some alternatives to nursing homes, and more may be available in the future. Already some ancillary services are at hand. Day hospices and hospitals relieve the strain on families. Wisconsin's Community Options Program is a model for many. For the past ten years it has held down the costs of long-term health care for thousands by allowing them to live on their own. A 1991 study by the Wisconsin Department of Health and Social Services found that COP and its comparable waiver services cost an average of $49.38 a day compared with $60.89 for Medicaid-financed nursing home care. COP also, for about $170 a month, provides an aide who does shopping, cleaning and laundry, and a lifeline pager linking with help should hospital care be needed.

Advocates of COP hope for flexible arrangements in which people can move back and forth between community and institutional settings, depending on their needs at the time, consolidating long-term health services into a single division at the state level. ADAPT, a Denver-based group, organized a lobbying drive of hundreds of disabled Americans, many in wheelchairs, in a demonstration near the Capitol on May 10, 1993, to shift federal dollars from nursing homes to in-home care for the elderly and disabled.

"The problem with health care reform is that the optimum system would include low costs, high quality and universal access," said Kim Hetsko, a Madison physician and former president of the State Medical Society. "We Americans want the best possible health care, want it immediately, and want someone else to pay for it."

Now, however, when there is almost universal reluctance to enter a nursing home, needy frail individuals are caught in a cruel bind; they badly need care they cannot afford. Alienation is more frequent for nursing home residents than for any other type of institutional residents. It may be that this end-of-life period, when one dwells between two worlds, not-here and not-there, is a rite of separation for which we have had no previous training. We sense that the most basic of human rights, that of making important choices about one's life and of determining where are our own best interests, are lost. We take pride in our independence, even when physically frail. Most pensions, small savings, and social security have convinced us we can manage somehow. Indeed, many do.

Nursing home care is an expensive proposition. Short-term frequently becomes long-term care. What is fearsome for many who have moved during their earning years is that catastrophic illness can wipe out savings quickly. Medicaid is possible, but to become eligible one must reduce resources. This means that no assets remain for a future return to normal living if that becomes clinically possible. In Dickens' day the poor dreaded the workhouse; Americans in the nineteenth and early twentieth century feared the poor farm. The name has changed, but the situation remains; the elderly become wards of the state, and they shrink from the thought. There is no easy way to veil the harshness, to soften the pain, to diminish the sadness.

As we grow older we are usually secure in a reasonably stable environment whose patterns are familiar enough so that skills and knowledge developed in the past can compensate for decreased functioning. A new environment can produce difficulties. We have seen friends who after moving to nursing homes, when confronted with major change, develop an unsettling loss in competence.

Theoretically we are protected from any arbitrary decisions being made for us. There are federal statutes which make it a criminal offense to force anyone to live where he does not want to go, and another which requires all health care providers who receive Medicare and Medicaid funding to provide patients with written information about their right to make decisions affecting their medical care. It is illegal to force that ultimate intrusion, guardianship, on anyone. The problem is that while the law safeguards the aged individual, when sick and virtually helpless such an individual cannot invoke a law which presupposes independence.

Recently I was an unwilling witness of the tragedy of choice and coping. I was a patient in the hospital, and an elderly woman, an accident victim, was brought into the room next to mine. Her husband had suffered a heart attack, crashed into a telephone pole, and died. She had suffered broken bones and bruises. Her life had suddenly collapsed around her, and she made little effort toward her own recovery. When it became obvious that she could not return to her home, doctors, social workers, her pastor, and neighbors (she had no living relatives) all tried to convince her of the necessity to go into a nursing home, even if temporarily, after her dismissal from the hospital. She refused, and by the time I was able to leave she had deteriorated and had been transferred to intensive care.

Although only one percent of aged Americans live in nursing homes, that adds up to almost two million residents. Almost always on entering the patient is emotionally exhausted. Preparations to move have included the sorting out of cherished belongings, since even if a private room is available—a rare exception in most nursing homes—it will be too small for any but the most limited possessions. What is devastating is when the choice of what to take is done by others who decide what the accommodations will allow: a couple of cartons, a half-dozen dresses or suits, a couple of shelves in a dresser. A lifetime in two boxes! A trunk will not be needed, nor a suitcase, since "they won't be going anywhere."

When older persons are involved as fully as possible every step of the way, there is less internal conflict, but even then the wrenching changes do take their toll. A quiet acceptance should not be mistaken for a happy stage. It is almost void of feeling, as if the pain has gone, the struggle is over, and a vacuum has taken their place.

Christ's words to St. Peter seem to be addressed to the individual at this stage. St. John records the incident which occurred after the resurrection. Jesus had put the three-times-repeated question, "Peter, son of John, do you love me?" and Peter had finally added to his protestation of love, "Lord, you know all things; you know that I love you." Then Jesus, after confirming Peter with "Feed my sheep," added the poignant prophecy, "I say to you, when you were younger you used to dress yourself and go where you wanted. But when you grow old, you will stretch out your hands, and someone else will dress you and lead you where you do not want to go." St. John adds: "He said this, signifying by what kind of death he would glorify God." For most of us aging followers it also signifies what manner of death will be ours, too, as we are led where we do not want to go.

It is common practice for patients to be interviewed and evaluated on admission to a nursing home. Questions are posed to determine if the patient is "with it" or not. Name? Age? Date? Most of us would find it difficult to answer the last if asked on the spur of the moment. But often enough, on the basis of this type of questioning a patient is categorized.

It is understandable that an institution must be run in an orderly manner, and that certain daily events must be scheduled. Reasonable as this is, it is one of the more trying aspects of this new institutional living. Having decisions made about the time to get out of bed, when to eat and what to eat, when to bathe and sometimes how often, what music to listen to and what TV programs to watch, can be seen as dehumanizing. A cartoon summarized this in an amusing way. A little old woman is responding to a health care person twice her size with, "Honey, I've been through two world wars, the great depression, taught 3,298 children, administered four elementary schools and outlived everyone of the people I worked with. I'm eighty-nine years old, and *you're* telling *me* it's *bedtime!*"

A great deal of improvement is needed in the approach

to older patients. Most of them prefer not to ask nurses for anything they can do themselves, but an unanswered call bell can drown trust and submerge hope.

There is no question that food in the rooms may attract vermin, but where does the nursing home resident go at midnight for something to eat? The last meal was seven hours ago; the next meal is seven hours in the future, and he is hungry now. Where to go for an aspirin for an "unscheduled headache," since aspirin isn't listed as a prescribed medicine? What about a cough drop for that scratchy throat?

On a lighter note, organized recreation can be satisfying to some and depressing to others. The bridge champion finds bingo less than exhilarating; the professional actor finds children's movies a bore. An elderly musician I know was exposed to reruns of Lawrence Welk, and experienced resentment from his roommate when he turned his own radio to the local FM station playing symphonies.

There is a whole new vocabulary to be learned. The nursing home resident learns that he needs intermediate or skilled care, that he does not suffer from insomnia but from sleep disorder, that pressure ulcers have replaced bedsores, and that he no longer takes medicine but has medications. There is no arguing away the humiliation of having to submit the body to the ministrations of others for its most intimate needs. How dehumanized care must seem when technical specialists appear to be more comfortable attending to the equipment than to the patient. And to be subjected to the special, low, carefully articulated speech used with very small children sends its message. It is no wonder that to many, adaptation to a nursing home is a stressful event.

Routine and efficiency are certainly important, but a quality of life may be lost when institutional needs are given precedence over people. The heavy impact of a barrage of life changes can be seriously destructive to the person, undermining, as they do, security and confidence in one's own judgement. Psychiatrists Thomas Holmes and Richard Rahe, authors of the famous stress scale, warn that too many changes, good or bad, in too short a time, create grave danger of emotional illness. It is not that the aging cannot face change. Nothing in their lives is unchanged at this point; what they need, perhaps, are grooves in which to relax and to gather strength lest they feel elbowed out of the human race. They may have moved only five miles from their homes, but it might as well be five thousand since all that is familiar is gone.

To help people maintain their individuality without compromising the needs of the group is a challenge, but somehow it must be done. John Berchmans, the young Jesuit later canonized, was asked on his deathbed what he had found most trying in religious life, and his answer is instructive: "Community life." He had chosen it. Many of the elderly have not, and their communal living comes at a time that all studies of personality show to be when the personal internal dimension is introversion, the turning of one's interest and attention inward rather than outward. This turning inward, Erikson believes, is a yearning for integrity rather than social withdrawal. But try to live a private life in a public place.

Adults who happen to be old are not different; they have just lived longer. They differ only in that, and a bit of emotional support can make them gratifyingly self-reliant in the new setting. I was told of an eighty-six year old who asked a much younger companion, "Are we walking too fast for you, dear?" Unneeded, undesired help carries its message of denigration, and is understandably resented.

Abraham was seventy-five when God told him to leave all and go into a strange land. When reminded of this, an elderly resident of a nursing home replied, "Yes, but he had Sarah."

Obviously, nursing home personnel cannot be expected to replace dead Sarahs, but an awareness of wounds hidden under brave assurances is itself a comfort and is usually sensed by the recipients. Textbooks tell students of geriatric nursing to "listen to the patient," but an acquaintance commented wryly, "I don't need someone to listen; I need someone to hear." Nursing home residents often have the conviction, justified or not, that they are crying into the void.

In many cases the doctor who has taken care of them for years is no longer available; the nursing home has its own staff doctor. He comes at regularly scheduled times, reads the charts, talks to the staff, signs medication orders, and may or may not see the patient if there is time. "If the charts are all right, the patient must be," may be the philosophy. Doctors have had a bad press for the past several years, and I do not want to join the critics. My personal experience has been exclusively of doctors who are capable, genuinely concerned professionals. But even they have admitted that this is not always the medical picture. Within the past month I have heard of two friends, both in nursing homes, who experienced almost callous indifference to their report of problems. It may have been that the doctors were preoccupied with a critically ill patient, were mentally rechecking prescribed treatment, or were just burned out. Whatever the reason, both incidents, while not actionable, helped build up frustration in the patients, which did not add to their well-being.

Caught in circumstances not self-guided, deprived of dear familiar trivialities, as well as the close human relationship of family, the nursing home resident feels cramped and confined in a situation for which he can envision no escape.

Some obtain strength by recalling that only God can make sense of this mess. And he does. He may seem distant at times, but as our human relationship to people changes with the years, so does that with God. It grows, even in the confusion and difficulty, and we experience the nearness. The road may still seem to be all downhill, but we can pray in the darkness, knowing that although we do not hear his answer, we are heard.

Are there no positives to nursing home living? Of course there are—and very substantial ones. Primarily, one is safe and secure in a well-built dwelling which is reasonably cool in summer and comfortably warm in winter, and served nourishing food on a regular schedule. These may be rather basic accommodations, but to the many who do not have them they are unattainable bliss. In January 1993 the media alerted the world to the tragedy of old people dying of cold and starvation in the unheated nursing home in war-torn Sarajevo, just down the road from UN headquarters. So many perished that it almost became an epidemic of death from freezing.

During the summer at least twenty-five of the home's residents were killed by sniper or mortar fire as they shuffled past windows or lay in their beds. While an official from the UN was visiting the home, an old man who was chopping wood in its courtyard suddenly collapsed, dead of a bullet to the head.

There is no running water in that nursing home, no electricity, and no hope.

Nursing homes in the United States have other advantages: a monitored health regimen with nursing care when needed, companionship, regular religious services in most. Some have chaplains who provide seminars, retreats, prayer sessions, and individual counseling. Laundry, hair care, and other personal services are provided, and usually there is a store which stocks toiletries and small luxuries.

Most nursing homes have both physical and occupational therapy departments, some music and art therapy. Programs, lectures, movies and other entertainment, both in the nursing home and outside, are available for those interested and able. Fewer and fewer are requiring attendance at programs as gerontologists stress the negative gain from such involuntary participation.

Holidays can be special events with well-prepared celebrations. Tickets for ball games, for theater, for civic celebrations are available in many, and transportation is provided either by the institution itself or by volunteers.

Hobbies are encouraged: woodworking rooms attract men as craft rooms do women. But they resent being exhibited, and rightly so. I was told of a resident in a woodworking room who was asked by a visitor what he was doing. "Whittling," was the laconic response.

"But what are you making?" the questioner insisted.

"Sawdust," the old man answered.

A goodly number of nursing homes function on the principle that it is not how old you are, but how you are old that matters. In these the residents find it easier to adjust when the end-of-life they had planned is not possible. Gradually they come to understand that the journey, like that of the Magi, has as its objective the meeting with Jesus, the ground of our being in every age. We can grow to see how everything in our lives, even living on this little island of time, makes complete sense.

When Alone But Not Lonely

Loneliness is a universal human phenomenon, and there is probably no one who has not felt lonely at some time. In fact, Sean Caulfield believes it may to some degree even be necessary, since it puts us in touch with our radical solitude, that center of our being. What makes this loneliness of the elderly different is that the emptiness grows out of a loss as well as a need. When more loved ones are dead than living, the emotion is one of isolation that any number of unfamiliar people cannot touch. In fact, all of us tend to pursue a separate loneliness in a crowd. The very pressures that impel us to come into community actually doom us to solitude, since we are individuals who cannot be fully understood. Because he was divine as well as human no one understood Christ; all his life he remained very much alone.

Existentialism, that twentieth century philosophy of nihilism, in which the individual, thrown into existence through no decision of his own, looks out to the galaxies and down the millennia in complete loneliness, can become very personal. Ladislaus Boros says that one of the most terrible experiences in a man's life is to complain, "I have no one." For the elderly, alone now, as never before, in inescapable solitude, things as well as people suddenly seem far removed.

Karl Rahner, dealing with sympathy and shared understanding of this situation of absolute loneliness when everything seems unreal, insists that the Christian who has

109

learned to pray can endure this silent, horrible emptiness. If we surrender to it we may experience that God is present in it. We may still cry, "I am, and nobody cares," but we sense that God is the one by whose caring I am. We are only because God thought of us, and we continue to exist only because of that divine concern. When Loren Eisely speaks of the human being as the cosmic orphan, if we listen we can hear the whispered response, "But I will not leave you orphaned."

Surrounded by the debris of our everyday lives, past the need for a healthy diet and vitamin pills, the work of the world no longer ours, we are finally empty enough for God to find room in our hearts, and the reality of that inner companion becomes evident. God is closer than we are to ourselves. He does not answer any questions; he simply fills the heart. Now we are able to find the right balance between being with others and being alone, since now we are never alone.

The elderly who experience this living reality do not become anti-social. On the contrary, their friends and relatives become more precious, but when they all leave, the elder person with a relaxed grasp returns to a deep and powerful silence in which he can find God. The relationship is no longer *to* God but *in* God. The early centuries of Christianity knew desert fathers who deliberately sought out solitude in the desert to establish a praying relationship with God. In every century since then there have been those who, even in crowded cities, have lived a simple, hermit-like experience. The elderly today frequently join that company, and in it discover personally that St. Theresa was right: God alone suffices. Their communion with him enables them to cope with the loneliness of old age.

Because liturgy for the house-bound and bedridden, precious though it is, can no longer be a frequent worship experience, God offers a substitute. After all, the sacraments are his gift, the means by which we draw closer to him, but he does not need them. For us it may be a time when formulas and rote prayers do not satisfy; even the well-beloved Lord's Prayer and the angelic tribute to Mary, when said at all, are lingered over in a kind of meditation. It is the inner prayer that transforms the whole hierarchy of values from the seen to the unseen, and fills the loneliness with presence.

"I used to talk to myself," said an eighty year old woman recently. "At least that is what thought is, isn't it? An internal ruminating. One day it struck me: God is within me. Why don't I talk with him? Now I have most personal and private conversations with him. I tell him anything; I even complain."

She is in good company, as are all those others who in the darkness express their bewilderment at their suffering and his apparent indifference. This cry at God's silence is found all through the psalms. They neither doubt nor despair; the very bitterness of their complaint arises from the psalmist's trust that God can do something if he chooses. Someone has pointed out that from the Babylonian exile to Auschwitz pious Jews have pleaded: I cry out by day and you answer not, by night and there is no relief for me. Christ, too, in the final tortured moments on the cross, called out from the same psalm, "My God, my God, why have you forsaken me?"

But even in the dark moments, when the aged, tired mind understands nothing, when faith is put to the test, the heart can be at peace. God can be trusted. He will explain the reasons for evil, sickness, suffering, and, yes, old age and death. But not now. There is a tender understanding of the human condition in Jesus' "... but you cannot bear it now."

Pascal's wager is not the answer. St. John of the Cross, the most quoted authority on the dark night of the soul, recognizes that below the level of consciousness is a recognition that none of these things separate us from God. When there is nothing left to cling to, we can say with St. Peter, "To whom shall we go? You have the words of eternal life." It has always seemed to me significant that Christ was not insulted by this almost desperate choice. He praises Peter for it.

In the new-found dialogue between God and the individual, something does happen, even when it seems like a monologue. There are fresh ways to pray. An elderly friend gathers the sorrowful mysteries into contemporary life, her own and the suffering world's. The agony in the garden for her joins Christ's abandonment with all in hospitals and nursing homes, in detention camps, and on battlefields. The scourging absorbs all the pain in the world, those agonizing from brutality and conflict both national and local, those with incurable diseases. In the crowning with thorns she links the insults and shame with all mental suffering in psychiatric wards, the less dramatic but equally devastating stress of the unemployed with families to support, the young with no foreseeable future, and the old who are terrified by what may happen. The carrying of the cross is for her the universal human condition, which even the wealthy, successful and powerful will eventually face, and for those unlikely recipients of charity she asks God's special charity. In the mystery of the crucifixion she faces death, her own and all who are dying. For her as for the Savior, that mystery blends imperceptibly into the resurrection with its glorious promise.

She has her own prayer approach to the joyful and glorious mysteries, with students, the newly married, babies and young people, all linked to the life of Christ.

A man whose business took him all over the world now

uses that world as his prayer focus. As he turns his globe slowly his fingers touch continents, countries, cities, battlefields and farms, oceans and playgrounds, and his prayers ask a blessing for all who live, work, play and suffer in them. His memory touches all those he knew in each place.

I have learned from another to use verbs for prayer: I love...I enjoy...I am grateful for...I belong to...God, Jesus, the Holy Spirit, Divine Providence. The mind and heart expand as the realization of what each connotes floods the consciousness. And then there is that marvelous one-word suggestion in the old medieval work, *The Cloud of Unknowing*. The anonymous writer reminds us that when the house is burning we do not say, "There is a conflagration in my building and assistance in extinguishing it would be appreciated." We shout, "Help, fire!" He suggests a similar word-arrow be aimed at the divine with the same intensity to pierce the cloud that separates us from him. Eastern mystics have used the formula in the mantra. To the Jews of the Old Testament God's name was seen as an extension of his person; if the divine name was invoked upon a country or person, they belonged in a special way to Yahweh. Christians who have with Christ called God Abba, Father, know what strength and comfort it gives. We sense the immanence of the infinite compassion which, as Sebastian Moore says, "realizes itself in a tortured world."

There are times when just observing beauty is enough to dispel loneliness. A field golden with waving wheat, a flowering plum tree in early spring, the explosion of light as the sun comes over the horizon, all expand the soul in wonder. But is it prayer? Is it not? Is our admiring an artist's work a satisfaction to him? Is complimenting the cook gratifying to her? Is cheering the home run evidence of our admiration? Appreciation is praise, and Mary underscored this truth when she sang, "My soul glorifies the

Lord," and then went on to list the wonderful things he had done for her, for Israel and for the world.

George MacDonald represents God saying to men, "You must be strong with my strength and blessed with my blessedness, for I have no other to give you."

One of the sources of that strength is scripture. Some of the books lend themselves more easily to a prayer response: Christ's words in the gospels, some of the prophets and the psalms. But there is more in the Bible than can be mined in one lifetime. Some years ago I was asked to compile words of comfort, consolation, and hope in scripture. The book when published was 191 pages, and I am sure I had not caught all the relevant phrases. Anyone can make a personal collection from any aspect of life; I plan to go through the holy book and gather words about this stage of my life. Some come to mind without effort—"But now that I am old and gray, O Lord, forsake me not" is an example—but I am sure there is an anthology for the ages hidden in the pages of both the Old and the New Testament.

Praying scripture, like all other prayer, presupposes a dialogue; we bring the passage which has personal meaning to God, and his response is often a revelation which enlarges its significance for our lives. Some years ago I inherited a Bible from a dearly loved friend who had died. The passages he had marked off expanded my concept of God's goodness, as what they must have meant to him became clear. I do not know if my prayer followed the lines his had, but his markings broke the trail for me.

Almost anything can become matter for this talking with God. A game my father and I used to play when I was a small child has, in my later years, become a scaffold for prayer for the unknown thousands of God's children who contribute to my well-being. My father would ask me how many people had worked to provide my breakfast, and as I went through the list from those who planted the corn, to those who harvested it, those who took it to the mill, the engineer of the train that took it to Battle Creek, and the many skilled laborers there who produced the Kellogg's Corn Flakes, I was made aware of the number of people outside the loving members of my own family to whom I owed even the simple things of life. Dad could always add names when I ran out of benefactors: "But what about the people who made the truck, the miners who brought up the coal, those who made the machinery? the paint? the boxes the corn flakes were packaged in?" And on, and on. Today I continue the childhood game at times, but I have added a new dimension. "God bless them all. Let them not be laid off; draw them close to you." It is an exercise in gratitude, not only to the nameless thousands but to God who brought my life and theirs together in this strange union.

Going back in memory to every place where one has lived, an exercise to which the aging are prone, can also be a platform for prayer. The Jesus prayer of the eastern mystics has become familiar to us. But it has always been in the Christian consciousness. "Jesus, Son of David, have mercy on me" was the cry that went out along the roads in Palestine as the messiah passed by, and we read of how instant was his response. Many use it today, moving on to what de Mello, Basil Pennington and others call the prayer of breathing, by which we breathe in the holy name, and breathe out the plea, "Mercy." Through it our very lives become a prayer, a direct, involved worship of God.

We have no control over the involuntary activities of our body, but we can direct them to their author. My congregation used to have a prayer we said before turning to sleep, in which we directed every breath and pulsation of our hearts during the night as an act of praise to the divine majesty. I do not know if the young sisters are still taught it, by many of us oldsters still say it.

At times things do crush in on us. Life is like that. Even the weather in sunny California has rainy days, and those in the midwest in the summer of the 1993 floods know the terror of mud slides, flash floods and sudden evacuation. There are such times in our prayer lives. I remember my sense of frustration during an illness when I had hours free for prayer, and yet, like Hamlet's uncle, my words went up, my thoughts remained below. I realize now that the very acknowledgement of my helplessness was a prayer, but at the time it was only an emptiness and loneliness. When people are in pain or exhausted by illness it is easy to become irritable and depressed.

Prayer is a kind of light that shows us what needs to be purified, and helps in the doing. We ask God to keep us from becoming cantankerous, self-opinionated, demanding old people. A priest friend recently shared his method of prayerful self-examination with me. He suggested going back to the moment of awakening, and going through the day with "Jesus and I woke up. Jesus and I dressed. Jesus and I went down to breakfast. Jesus and I argued with ..." No, that's wrong. Jesus and I didn't argue; I did it all alone.

As our prayer deepens we are aware that while our daily lives may seem to be dull and monotonous, they are not unimportant to the God who has counted our every hair. So, in faith, we do not resist our aging process; we go with it. And sometimes, in the midst of our babbling prayer, we hear interiorly the voice that thundered on Sinai, "Be still, and know that I am God." And we are quiet in that knowledge. Isaiah had the message right. "The mountains may fall, the hills be shaken, but my love for you will never leave you, and my covenant of peace with you will never be shaken. What more do you want? You shall see what I intend to do for you."

We do not know what the future holds, but we know who holds the future. We can relax in that knowledge. Weston Priory has a hymn that expresses our emotion in this surge of faith that destroys loneliness: You fill the day with your glory and your power; you fill the night with your quiet and your deep, deep love.

When We Prepare for the
Final Journey

It was Thomas Edison, I believe, who said, "I am long on ideas, and short on time." For all of us the moment comes when we realize that we, too, are short on time, and for those who have confounded the actuarial tables already, the moment is one of immediacy. Dying is not far in the future; the body gives its own notice that the end is near. Older people do not appear to be extremely afraid of death; in fact, they express fewer death fears than younger ones, probably because they have fewer lingering responsibilities. The young man or woman worries about family, about finances, about how much the sickness is costing. And those are justifiable worries. My father was in the hospital for three weeks some fifty years ago, and the total bill was $1,500. His mother, twenty-five years before that, had special care, with round-the-clock private nursing, for $50 a week. A pharmacist's bill can amount to more than that today.

A Gallup poll taken among centenarians found that they had a positive attitude toward life, and a basic indifference to death. Psychiatrist Hattie Rosenthal explains it as the result of a full life, leaving the individual with comparatively little anxiety and a readiness to die.

But we really do not know much about dying, or what the dying think, in spite of extensive studies in the area. It is the loneliest thing we shall ever do. We shall all experience it, but it is not an experience we can share. The dying do not talk much, and famous last words are not particularly illuminating. Even geniuses tend to sound ambiguous and banal, and Goethe's famous "More light" may mean many things. We do not know what Goethe really meant by them.

Ascetical writers tell about the people who live to a peaceful, ripe old age, but there is also the sort of old age that steadily and inexorably draws near to death, an old age in which there is loss of vital life energy, in which one is simply exhausted. Christians must cope with this old age, too, without illusion, because we do have hope, and the terrible death of Christ is our reason for hope. Death is part of that whole miasma of evil in which man has become bogged down, and from which Jesus came to liberate us.

A great deal has been written about the stages people go through in the process of dying. Dr. Elisabeth Kübler-Ross in 1969, after studying a number of terminally ill patients, proposed five stages: denial, anger, bargaining, depression, and acceptance. But this is not an inevitable and invariable progression. There is a wonderful story, perhaps apocryphal, about a young doctor who was disturbed that a patient he was treating was near death and apparently had not gone through all the stages. When he told Kübler-Ross of his concern, she answered, "Perhaps they went by so fast you missed them."

How does one deal with the message of death? Since each of us dies his or her own death in supreme loneliness, it would be presumptuous to assert anything universal about that individual moment of trial.

I know how I faced it some years ago. The evening before surgery which I had thought would be uneventful, a specialist came into my room to explain in great detail the risks I would be undergoing the following day. When I finally found my voice to say "Are you telling me I should not have agreed to this?" he answered, "No, no, of course not. You need it, or you would be incapacitated. I'm just warning you of the possible complications."

When he left I did not go through Kübler-Ross' five stages. I found myself repeating in a kind of numb wonder, "Now—at the hour of my death," a kind of prayer, over and over again. I did not deny; I was not angry. I did not dwell on the unfinished business others would have to take over; I did not even think of the fact that I was alone at this decisive moment, nor that I might not be saying goodbye to those I love. There was room only for the one thought: "Now—at the hour of my death." Everything else was inconsequential everything was compressed in that phrase: my love of life, my trust in God, everything. Eventually the pre-surgical hypo took over, and I was awakened the next morning to be gurneyed up to the operating room. Obviously, since I did not die, this example would seem to have no relevance. How I will react when the reality again faces me is hidden in the future.

This autumn a sister here at the Health Care Center fell and broke her hip. As the ambulance door closed she said to us, "I won't be back." Today hip surgery is a rather routine procedure, but she was right. She did not come back, except for her funeral. How did she know? How did she handle the knowledge? That is her secret, and she took it with her.

Some years ago I was witness to one of the loneliest of deaths, a prototype of many in today's world. Our bursar in Italy received a call from the Roman coroner. The name and address of a sister in our congregation was on a slip of paper found in the suit of a vagrant who had died on the street the night before. Sister remembered the name as that of a man who claimed to be an American in exile, out of work, out of luck, and out of money. Sister had helped him, and obviously he has listed her and our convent as a place he might call on again if needed. He had died alone, and since he had no known friends or relatives in Italy he would be buried in a pauper's grave. We told the coroner to arrange the funeral; we would be present. We asked for the dead man's size, intending to buy a suit for his burial, but were told he would be wrapped in a sheet and laid in a common grave. A suit would not be needed; we could give it to the living poor. We who did not know him were the only mourners at the funeral mass, the only ones who went to his burial. I have often wondered whether he realized at the end that he was dying, and how he handled that knowledge, alone.

Kübler-Ross has pointed out that dying in our society can also be lonely, mechanical and dehumanized, with the patient out of his familiar environment, surrounded by strangers, all of whom are doing their duty, none of whom loves him for himself, or even knows him as a person.

Most older people share a common emotion: I would not be afraid of dying if I knew what I would have to go through before death comes. We all resonate to that shrinking, for we have our own picture of the long, lonely hours before the tired heart stops. Health care personnel are often so busy monitoring the heart rate, pulse, and pulmonary functions that they may forget that they are dealing with a human being still in need of reassurance and a human touch.

Most physicians do not believe they can predict death accurately. I recall the look of gratitude in a relative's eyes as her doctor said, "I've done all I can to help you. But don't worry; I'll keep you as comfortable as possible."

Communication at the end becomes more non-verbal than verbal. The dying drift off, with intermittent awareness. A "don't disturb me" look is a barrier between them and the living. Those who have cared for the dying observe that in the majority of cases a moment comes when pain ceases to dominate, when the eyes close and the mind rests, and a silence beyond words settles in the sickroom, a moment that is not at all frightening. God's power seems to take over at the moment of mortal powerlessness.

In the year I have been at our retirement home thirty-two sisters who were residents here when I came have gone to God, the majority in their eighties or older. Their deaths were not "easy"—death seldom is—but neither were they dreadful. The deaths I have witnessed in a long lifetime have been a quiet release. Nurses I have talked with agree that the end is almost never frightening. Hospice nurses Maggie Callahan and Patricia Kelley recently wrote an instructive book on their experience with dying patients: *Final Gifts* (Poseidon Press, 1992) in which they detail the comfort that the dying give those who care for them. Some share a "near-death" experience which dispelled anxiety and left them with an unusual calm, an eagerness to go.

The dying have ways of communicating other than words; their behavior and actions show us what they are experiencing. They reach out for someone or something unseen, smile, wave, nod, or attempt to talk with someone invisible to others. Although these actions seem inappropriate and are often interpreted as confused behavior, they indicate that the individual is experiencing something.

Sometimes, and usually without warning, some patients muster unusual strength. It would appear that they see someone invisible to us. Some even manage to get out of bed if left alone. Callahan and Kelley feel that they are responding to a call no one else can hear. We cannot know, but the consistency of near-death experience cannot be ignored.

While there are some patients who do not want to be told that they are dying, there is an equal number who keep their prognosis secret. It would seem that the majority know of their impending demise, whether they have been told of it or not. Their expression of that knowledge may be oblique so that we miss it. "I am going home." "It is almost time." "What are we waiting for?" "I'm ready." "Please sit down; tomorrow may be too late."

My father, hours before his death, said to my mother and me with an amused smile, "You girls had better make reservations to stay in this hotel tonight."

A diagnostician in a large urban hospital was being treated for a broken shoulder when it was discovered he was suffering from advanced bone cancer. When he asked to see his X-rays he examined them carefully, then passed them to his young colleague with, "I'd give that one about a week, wouldn't you?"

A very sick woman who played the game of superficial conversation with visitors was asked by one who had witnessed the exchange, "Do you ever think that you may not recover?" The answer was a quiet, "My death is constantly in my mind."

There are hundreds of ways in which people signal or sign, although there is not a lot of stark talk about dying. Some do not seem to mind dying, but their bodies do. They withdraw, unable to tell us what it is like, and that is understandable. We handle important things badly in words. Practically no one introduces the topic; people talk about their arthritis, or the pancakes they had for supper.

In spite of moving deathbed passages in novels, inspiring messages rarely occur in real life. I was a young nun when an old sister who had been principal in the school where I was teaching became critically ill. She gathered all of us around for a "farewell message," and then spoke to each individually in what I remember as a moving experi-

ence. I was young and impressionable, and this was certainly a "happy death." Sister lived another twenty years,
and was in a coma at the time of her actual death. No
drama, no message.

And yet there can be emotional experiences in the final
goodbye. Last Christmas I visited a former colleague in an
oncology hospice. He had been a navy officer, a
Shakespearean actor, a scholar, and for thirty years in our
college had taught classes which were both demanding
and popular. When I saw him the physical buoyancy was
gone, but the spiritual and mental dynamism was still in
control. His doctor, suggesting chemotherapy and radium
treatments, had been frank in stating that they might not
be effective. Ed's response must have startled the doctor.
"Let's go for it," he said. "I'm in a no-lose situation. If the
treatment works, I've won. If it doesn't, I'm a Christian,
and I know I've won."

The day I saw him it was evident the disease was beyond
treatment. He did not skirt the issue. "The doctor says I
have no more than three months to live. Which means
January, February, March. April would seem to be a good
month for a memorial service; you'll be getting an invitation. Everything is ready."

He died less than six weeks later, and at that memorial
service two of the hospice nurses spoke, telling what a joy
it had been to take care of that man.

But what of those of us who do not face this peak experience with similar equanimity? Many suppress their interi-
or repugnance, their fear, because they feel that these indicate a character flaw. Shakespeare underscored the attitude in the famous, "Cowards die many times before their
death; the valiant only taste of death but once." This time,
though, Shakespeare is wrong. We have a right to be
afraid. Fear of death is not forbidden us; Jesus' agony was
a dreadful wrestling with the same fear. One translation of

scripture says he was terrified, and both Matthew and Mark have him crying, "My soul is sorrowful, even unto death." Daniel Berrigan tells of a young man dying in the hospital for the sick poor who said, "I don't see how Jesus could have borne the crucifixion."

But he died, and in that terrible death of Jesus our faith is rooted. Jesus crucified and risen is our hope, for we know that our redeemer lives, and in our flesh we shall see him. He has promised to be with us to the end of the world, our personal world, which is death. He gives himself to us as our eternal life. We believe that, because of him, our own life will be changed, not taken away.

We are not asked to deny that death is terrible weakness, crushing solitude, when everything slips away. It is a frightening happening, and fear of death is universal, even when we may think we have mastered it. Underneath, we have an assurance that keeps surfacing: that this is the fulfillment of life, the end that gives meaning to everything that has been.

On the cross Jesus has taken up our protest against death and justified it. The crucifixion does not answer our questions it simply quiets them. It emphasizes the truth that, as someone has said, while only God can raise the dead, even God can *only* raise the dead. Jesus' death destroyed death; we have his word for it.

We struggle to overcome death by seeing God there, but because in many cases there is a slipping into unconsciousness, a kind of stupor of dying, many of us strive to make God's moment ours while we still have some control. We make a personal, strong decision of love now, so that what Boros calls "the sacrament of dying" may be the ultimate grace.

There is the sacrament of anointing which also addresses this culmination of our personal human existence. This ritual emphasizes our participation in the paschal mystery, and while today it is no longer "extreme unction," it still carries more than a hint of mortality. We can entrust ourselves to God; Christ's own resurrection was preceded by powerlessness, and while the sacrament of the sick does not always guarantee a return to health, it does guarantee the miracle of a new life in God. It is the sacrament of hope, and, together with the eucharist, brings the grace to overcome anxiety and despair.

A dimension to the whole question of dying is the ethical issue of the right to die. How long must we sustain the artificial life supports that maintain the vital functions and drag out the moment of departure? Direct euthanasia is out of the question for Christians, but we have the right to indicate that we do not want unusual life supports at the end. The Patient's Bill of Rights, approved by the American Hospital Association in 1973, assures us that we will be given complete information about diagnosis, treatment and prognosis. Predictability contains its own comfort, and because we do not want extraordinary or heroic measures to be taken to prolong the act of dying, the wise among us have signed a living will with written instructions concerning medical treatment in case of terminal illness or irreversible conditions, and we have filed this, as well as a power of attorney for health and care decisions, with our physicians.

I recall a friend telling me about being admitted to the hospital on an emergency basis rather late at night. By the time the necessary measures had been taken it was well past midnight. The IV's were functioning; the oxygen had been adjusted, the monitor checked, and a pain-killer administered. She was drifting off into drowsy unconsciousness when a resident came in with an important question: "Sister, if you go into cardiac arrest tonight, what measures do you want us to take?" It was a startling question at two in the morning.

The moment of awareness of death will come to every human being, the moment when we come face to face with its thrust into the unknown reality. It is the falling away of limits, the primordial collapse of our hold on life when everything will be swept away. John says that the dead will hear the voice of God in that moment, and like Mary Magdalene in the garden they will recognize him as he calls their name.

But we, the living watchers, must also listen. A nurse reported that onlookers occasionally speak of the dying person as "out of it," or "not quite right anymore." Even when they are too weak to speak, or seem to have lost consciousness, they can hear, since hearing appears to be the last sense to fade. The dying do separate themselves, little by little, from everything, even from loved ones. This is not indifference. Jesus' relationship with his friends after the resurrection was different but real. We hope for a more extensive communion with our own than we have ever been able to achieve on earth. How wonderful it will be to recognize our ancestors, to know our grandparents as people with stories to tell of God's gifts to them, and their achievements with his help. While everything seems to be slipping away forever, we believe that everything of value is safe in the fullness of God. We are dust, but into no other dust did he breathe his Spirit.

When the last resources of personhood are exhausted, we can calmly let go and permit God's gentle power to take over for us, in this the sum of all our diminishments. People who have had the near-death experience all report an all-wise, all-loving light that beckons them: a life-affirming newness seems to envelop them, and they can let go of the present.

One last thing—we ought to watch with the dying when we can. It is difficult; we feel we cannot do anything, but our presence blesses. Mary could do nothing for her dying

Son, but she stood there, and his word to her indicated his awareness of all she brought to that hill of horror.

We did not choose the moment of our birth, and we do not choose the moment of our death. But we can, with Jesus, offer ourselves to the Father as his, now while we can choose. Don Pedro Arrupe, S.J., father general of the Jesuits, covered it all in a prayer he wrote a month before he was stricken by the cerebral hemorrhage that eventually took his life. He wrote: "In reality, death, which is sometimes feared so much, is for me one of the most anticipated events, an event that will give meaning to my life. Death can be considered as an end of life or as a threshold of eternity; in both of these aspects I find consolation. As the end of life, it is still the end of a life that is nothing else than a path crossing a desert to approach eternity... Inasmuch as death is also the threshold of eternity, it involves the entrance into an eternity that is at the same time unknown and yet longed for; it involves meeting the Lord and an eternal intimacy with Him...What will Heaven be like? It is impossible to imagine. I hope that it will be a *consummatum est*—all is finished, the final Amen of my life and the first *Alleluia* of my eternity. *Fiat, fiat* (Be it done, be it done)."[1]

[1] Reprinted with permission of America Press, Inc., 106 West 56th Street, New York, NY 10019. ©1991. All rights reserved.

And Finally ...

It has been a year since I came face to face with my own chronological-biological age and my imminent mortality. It is ten months since I came to live in this, my congregation's retirement home, with my sisters, for all of whom the years have been an eroding force. While my own health remains relatively stable, I have watched companions become weaker, finally letting slip the fragile threads that bind them to earth.

If this book seems to stress the difficulties that frequently accompany aging, I make no apologies. It is a time of diminishment, and a shallow optimism does not alter the fact. Perhaps my perspective has grown out of the fact that I live surrounded by ambiguities, by profound and irrevocable changes. I am in the dual position of being both an observer and a participant; I stand between those who have ceased to plan because they know that while they have today they may not have tomorrow, and those whose personal agenda stretches far into the future. But what is common to us all is our humanity. This is true even for those who have problems with mobility and cognition and whose restrictions of independent functional ability have reached the point where they cannot handle their own most personal needs.

Being old forces one to face the final questions of life; our bodies present it rigorously, and our personal answer is demanded. Shadowed though this end of life may be, it is not totally grim. I have witnessed fortitude and graciousness, joy, pleasure, and merriment. C.S. Lewis once said that our Father refreshes us on the journey with some pleasant inns, but will not encourage us to mistake them for home. Meister Eckhart noted that God enjoys himself and wants us to enjoy with him. The retired sisters with whom I live, aware as they are that each morning is a special gift, have a capacity for enjoyment unequaled by any other group with whom I have lived. Theirs is the relaxed grasp. They treasure small moments: a visit from a friend, a letter, a photograph of a new baby, a bowl of flowers on a shining mahogany table. They enjoy an occasional treat—a ride in the park, fireworks against the horizon, a concert.

Those with brain damaging disease may show personality change, but the majority of us carry into our twilight years the same gifts and impediments we always had. The possibility of spiritual growth remains, even when the body deteriorates. I have witnessed an eye for others' needs, an awareness and concern for others' weakness, coupled with unobtrusive help offered, help which the willing young simply do not see because they themselves are self-sufficient. Those whose lives have been filled with service continue within the parameters of their ability. One of my peers continued to help in a local soup kitchen until a few weeks before her death. Another has made hundreds of layettes for the unwed mothers' hospice, and several continue to use their skills as teachers. A party may have cookies a retired cook has baked.

I have seen a patient with multiple sclerosis push the wheelchair of a recovering surgical patient, another, herself crippled by arthritis, lead a near-blind friend through the maze of dining room chairs, and another with inoperable cancer carry the tray of a palsied sister with Parkinson's. These are survivors who have learned to cope in their shrinking world. As one said, "We may need help getting from place to place, but we know more than we have ever known about making good choices.

Expectations and requirements become smaller as boundaries narrow. There is a tendency to encourage the elderly to look at the bright side of life, at all the colorful, positive things around them. This is often an expression of the caretaker's needs; the elderly do not have to be reminded of the obvious. Two letters I received just this week underscore acceptance.

A recently retired friend, a professor for many years, wrote, "I expect to enjoy life for a few more years. Last Thanksgiving I decided to retire, and have not regretted doing so."

A ninety year old woman wrote, "God is good to spare our mental faculties, no matter how creaking and cramping our bodies seem. We have a small discussion group that gathers informally in the evening just for fun. Our talk is of shoes and ships and sealing wax and cabbages and kings."

Those two have learned to accept bravely and without self-pity the harshness that is a part of life, together with its vitality, strength, and glory. And that acceptance is only achieved when one is in union with God.

I have seen what the grace of the Holy Spirit has accomplished in these, the beloved servants. At Pentecost I had my own sudden revelation as, reflecting on the gifts of the Spirit, I suddenly realized that they were daily embodied in those about me. I have seen love, joy, peace, patience, tenderness, goodness, faith, modesty and continence in living action daily in the elderly with whom I live. They demonstrate that for them, and for all of us, Christian faith transforms these last decades of life. We become aware that the goodbye at the end of a visit may be just that.

I have listened to theological discussions on prayer that were a casual part of conversation. "Sometimes I feel

Jewish," commented one companion. "At this time of my life I seem to prefer prayers of praise to those of petition. I like the song of Daniel in which he brings everything into the canticle of worship. You remember: sun, moon, stars, shower, dew, winds, fire, heat, cold, chill, ice, snow, nights and days. I always end up a little breathless."

I recently overheard another wondering about the prayer of petition. "I have a problem," she said. "When I beg God to help someone it seems to imply I care more for the person than he does, and that he needs to be reminded. Jesus said, 'Your Father knows you have need of these things.' "

"That's true," was her friend's answer, "but he also taught us the Our Father, and he himself prayed for people. Anyway," she added, "God may not need to be reminded of our needs, but I need to be reminded of my relationship to people, and praying for them does just that."

And how they pray! The morning paper becomes an agenda for the day. Every local, national or world crisis is matter for petition. Every sick relative or friend is named to God. Every evening one of my sisters sits in the chapel, and what she is saying to God remains her secret, but I envy her absorption. People may come or go; she remains totally absorbed.

There are sad moments too, of course. When one shares the news that her diagnosis is cancer there is genuine concern. When another announces an impending operation there is the promise of prayer. The greatest sorrow is when one of our number leaves for the nursing home; we all gather for the departure, and the loss is heavy for days. Part of it unquestionably is the gnawing suspicion that we may be the next to go, but all sympathize with a friend who leaves the familiar forever.

It is in the dark times that we cling to the one who

changes things at their root, who promised that the eyes of the blind would be opened and the ears of the deaf unsealed, that the lame would leap like a deer and the tongues of the dumb sing for joy. We know that he shines "on those who dwell in darkness and the shadow of death, and guides our feet into the way of peace."

That is why, even when the air is colder and sharper, the road more desolate, we can still say with Dag Hammarskjold,

You set my foot upon the road; the end I cannot guess.
For all that has been, thanks; for all that shall be Yes.